"Just Came By To Tell You..."

[signature]

"Just Came By To Tell You..."

Copyright © 2012 by the family of G. W. Lane
Library of Congress Control Number: 2012943539

G. W. Lane 1912 — 1982
"Just Came by to Tell You"
ISBN 978-1-935434-11-5

Subject Codes and Description: 1: REL012000: Religion: Christian Life - General 2: REL012040: Religion: Christian Life - Inspirational 3: REL006980: Religion: Christian Life.

This book is presented by the family of G. W. Lane in collaboration with GlobalEdAdvancePress. All rights reserved, including the right to reproduce this book or any part thereof in any form, except for inclusion of brief quotations in a review, without the written permission of GlobalEdAdvancePRESS.

Printed in Australia, Brazil, France, Germany, Italy, Spain, UK, and USA

Cover Design by Barton L. Green

The Press does not have ownership of the contents of a book; this is the author's work and the author owns the copyright. All theories, concepts, constructs, and perspectives are those of the author and not necessarily the Press. They are presented for open and free discussion of the issues involved. All comments and feedback should be directed to the Email: [comments4author@aol.com] and the comments will be forwarded to the author for response.

Published by
Clergy Collections
a subdivision of Post-Gutenberg Books
GlobalEd AdvancePress
a division of
Global Educational Advance, Inc.

Dedication

"...to my wife, Nellie, and daughter, Peggy, who were faithful co-workers in all my efforts in the ministry. ...to my grandson, Barton, with a hope that he will grow to know the Lord and love Him intimately. ...to my grandson, Brian, with a prayer that he will depend upon the Word of God as his compass throughout life."

~

The sermons in this collection were taken from
earlier works by G. W. Lane
The Voice of Calvary, But This Man, and *Bring the Book*

G. W. and Nellie Boman Lane

Table of Contents

Tributes	11
Preface	17
1. Parade of the Ages	20
2. Message of the Burning Bush	28
3. Double Resting Place	38
4. Great Surprise	48
5. Shallow Water	58
6. Voice of Calvary	70
7. Perfect Law of Liberty	80
8. Altar to the Unknown God	90
9. Forgotten Prophecy	100
10. Cost of Compromise	110
11. Lift of Life	120
12. This Waiting World	132
Honor	141

Tributes

I am very proud to endorse the release of *"Just Came By To Tell You..."* The Collected Works of G.W. Lane, Volume 1. I remember as a child going with my grandfather as he ministered on the weekends. I would sit on the front pew to watch Papaw sing and preach and many times at 8, 9, 10 years old, found myself moved to tears...You know, children can sense if the truth is being told. That truth still resonates with me today.

Recently, he was inducted into the 'Hall of Prophets'....kind of like the 'Rock and Roll Hall of Fame' for the sacred world. People came from all over the country for the ceremony that honored his life's work. He made an impact on so many lives.... and with this new collection his ministry continues.

-Brian Lane Green

*****

From my youth I have always considered G.W. Lane my father in the Lord. I can remember so many times preaching one of his sermons and he would come to hear me. Unless he was already scheduled to be somewhere else he would come.

On one occasion, I was preaching Lane's, *"I Met The Master"* in a camp meeting and he was the liaison from the denomination's Executive Committee that night. Paul Barker was in attendance, turned to Bro. Lane and said, "He's preaching one of yours and doesn't even know it."

"Oh, he knows it," Lane smiled, "But he has preached my stuff so much he thinks it's his." He always felt it was the greatest compliment one could give him.

I loved him so much and missed him so when he was gone. I developed a habit of calling him every Saturday and had the phone in my hand dialing his number when it occurred to me, "…he isn't here."

I was asked to write a paragraph but it is so hard to limit words to just one when it seems I could write a book about him.

-Floyd Lawhon

*****

While only the celebrations of heaven will reveal the fruits of the ministry of Reverend G.W. Lane, I have witnessed first hand the impact of his ministry in my personal life. He was the pastor of the 12th and Elm Church in Cincinnati Ohio and officiated at the baby dedication service when I was dedicated.

Eventually, the church moved to its present location on Central Parkway, Cincinnati, Ohio and he left to became a State Overseer and then General Secretary and Treasurer for the denomination.

By the time I was a teenager, I was operating the soundboard for the 'Parkway's' services from a remote room overlooking the sanctuary. Often Brother Lane (who by then served on the Executive Committee) would stop by. Being that he was travelling frequently then, it was not uncommon for Brother Lane to take a respite from the road and ease by the church on Sunday nights after service had begun. He would slip in not to be seen or draw attention. The door to the sound room would quietly open and he would appear. Lane would stand back where he would not be seen and survey the congregation, looking to see who was in attendance. Then he would sit down, and briefly inquire as to the individuals he didn't see in service and the current events of the church. Then, Lane would quietly, poignantly share stories and detailed experiences from his ministry as pastor in Cincinnati.

His stay was always brief, yet purposeful. As the service was coming to an end, he would slip back out and head home undetected by those in church that night.

Little did I know that what he had just came by to tell me was preparing me for the ministry which God would later call me to; the very pastorate he once served at the Central Parkway!

-Ron K. Martin

*****

As a third generation Church of God preacher, I have a deep appreciation for our heritage and for those who have helped pave the way for me to be able to minister in this great movement. I am thankful that my grandfather and father preserved their old Camp Meeting tapes and passed them down to me.

Among my favorites are the messages preached by Rev. G. W. Lane. Very few men have inspired me the way Bro. Lane has. His fire, passion, and anointing made him different than most preachers we hear today. If I can describe his preaching in one word it would be "alive." Every time I listen to his sermons "God the Word," "I Met the Master," and my favorite, "Not Many Days Hence", I am stirred by the powerful anointing through which he preached. Being a thirty-one year old preacher and too young to have ever seen him preach in person, I feel as if God raised up this man not only for his generation but for mine as well.

We could learn a great deal from this great pioneer of the faith. My prayer is that I can impact a young preacher's life well after I have passed on to my reward as much as G. W. Lane has impacted me.

-Michael A. Ball

*****

In his sermons, the Reverend G. W. Lane sets forth that the Bible provides for man's total need. The sermons vividly portray that God cares for each individual and that there is a Divine way to happiness and an abundant entry into the Christian way of life.

Thousands around the world have come under the influence of G. W. Lane's dynamic preaching and joyful singing. His printed and published sermons extended the influence of his ministry. This volume of his best messages will continue to bless a new generation. This book presents a selected group of memorable sermons which convey the vigorous faith and consistent efforts of the Reverend Mr. Lane to give the Holy Bible the proper place in the heart and the lifestyle of followers of Christ.

This is a frenzied world. There are many hucksters on the streets attempting to sell their wares. Various panaceas are being offered as a sure cure to humanity's many ills. To risk any one man-made remedy or a combination of such, as a means to attain answers to our questions and satisfaction of our desires is dangerous and deadly. The hope of the world is to be found in the Bible – the Book of Books. May this book inspire you to lay hold of peace and strength through the Word of God.

-R. Leonard Carroll, Ed.D. from *Bring the Book*

*****

There is a stimulating variety of good preaching here. The reader will be blessed and encouraged. Besides these conscious benefits, there will also be a strengthening in the Christian way of life. Here is preaching that exalts Christ and reveals the heart and soul of the Reverend G. W. Lane.

For a good number of years I observed with appreciation the effective ministry of G.W. Lane. His preaching was noted for its powerful simplicity and his pastorate for its remarkable evangelism. The harvest of this ministry was abundant in conversions and spiritual growth. In addition to his pastoral and administrative duties, author Lane was much in demand for camp meetings and evangelistic campaigns. His radio and TV ministry won a tremendous following in America, and in many parts of this hemisphere.

It is a pleasure to introduce a book of such sound and sincere sermons. In a day of much preaching and many Christian books, there is a lack of preaching that has the true ring of the Christian gospel. There is a need for preaching that is sound because it is set in the Word of God and that is eloquent because of its earnestness. This is a book of such sermons.

-Dr. Charles W. Conn from *The Voice of Calvary*

The Lane family during the "Voice of Calvary" years

Preface

Many around the world came under the influence of the powerful preaching and energetic singing of G. W. Lane. In addition to being an effective preacher and singer, Lane was also able to communicate through the printed page. The sermons in this book are taken from the manuscripts used on the "Voice of Calvary" broadcast, and were often distributed through a program known as The Lane Line.

Part of GEA's new "Clergy Collection" series, *Just Came By To Tell You...* is designed to not only celebrate Lane's Centennial Year, but to also preserve these remarkable messages for a new generation and be a significant addition to Lane's list of published works.

These inspiring sermons convey the vigorous faith and consistent effort of the Reverend Lane to give the Bible the proper place in the heart and soul of believers, and enable them to witness through a Christian lifestyle. Lane believed the Bible was the foundation of knowledge and God's message to bring individuals into fellowship with Christ. He was certain that the written Word was the inspiration and the imperative for all of life's pursuits.

Beginning his career in his native Texas, Lane ministered as an evangelist, pastor, state youth director, and served as overseer of multiple states. Given his dynamic voice, his ministry flourished as the speaker for Cincinnati's national radio broadcast, "Voice of Calvary" and later as the radio/TV minister for the denomination's international outreach "Forward In Faith."

He served his denomination as General Secretary/Treasurer and as a member of the Executive Council. During his ministry, Lane published several volumes with titles; such as, *Doctrine of the New Testament, Program and Purpose, Material for Ministers, Sermon Nuggets, Pentecostal Persuasion, Bring the Book, But This Man,* and *The Voice of Calvary.*

During Lane's active ministry, he often began a message with the greeting, "Just came by to tell you…" This book is an effort to "Preserve the Best" of what he "came by" to say.

1

Parade of the Ages

"On the next day much people that were come to the feast, when they heard that Jesus was coming to Jerusalem, took Branches of palm trees and went forth to meet him, and cried, Hosanna: Blessed is the King of Israel that cometh in the name of the Lord."

(John 12.12, 13)

Every city and town has enjoyed the excitement of parades from school bands to celebrities traveling down the streets between great lines of enthusiastic onlookers. Most of them have little meaning and are to be enjoyed only as long as they last. This parade of one man riding on an donkey through the streets of Jerusalem was one of the greatest importance. It was the opening exercise of a week of world-shaking events.

Little did Christ's disciples think that the march into Jerusalem would be any different to their other visits there, neither did they know that the program of this parade had been outlined in writing five hundred years before, that God had spoken to Zechariah the prophet and inspired him to write in Zechariah 9:9, "Rejoice greatly, O daughter of Jerusalem behold, thy King cometh unto thee: he is just, and having salvation: lowly and riding upon an ass, and upon a colt the foal of an ass."

Centuries had passed and this writing held no special meaning to anyone. It had slipped out of their minds that such had been said, but God never forgets His plan or His schedule. His timetable is ever before Him and with or without the knowledge of the world, God keeps His schedule. God works on precision basis, He never fails in His purpose, and His plans do not go adrift.

It probably would be interesting to note that God had arranged this event in every detail centuries before the little mule He was to ride or it's owner ever lived. The owner of the beast did not know of the event; He just staked him out as usual on this day. Jesus sent two disciples to bring the ass, saying, "If anyone asks you about it, just tell them the Lord hath need of him." God does not ask questions of anyone when it is time to work.

I am reminded of Saul, who became the first king of Israel, when Israel desired a king. Saul was out searching for his mules that were lost. God spoke to Samuel and said, "Today a man will come to you in search of his mules. He is my choice for king Israel, anoint him." He came on schedule as a farmer, and left as the king of Israel.

In the same manner of absolute procedure so beautifully portrayed in this account, God continues to work. Kings and dynasties may change, emperors may be succeeded, national leaders may come and go, but that which is planned for the world you may count on being carried out in every detail and schedule.

It is possible that camels were plentiful, and carriages were available for this ride through the city, but God had planned for a ride on the ass and there could be no change. This operation in minute detail is the means by which the disciples were made to realize they were seeing a fulfillment of prophecy before their eyes. "Then remembered they that these things were written of him, and that they had done these things unto him."

The world may forget the voice of God and the plan of God, but just as surely as God has spoken, you can count on the fulfillment. He sent the owner to stake out the ass for the parade. He sent Saul to Samuel for his anointing as king, but today the nations of the world are on stage acting out the great drama of God's word in prophecy. The rulers are unaware that the outline of history is pre-written but a search in God's word would bring to their knowledge the fact that God's schedule is being kept and the nations are a part of the program.

The majority of today's population like the multitudes of people on the day we are commemorating are unaware of the importance of the issues of today, and the part they play in an age fast coming to a close. Only those close to Jesus could comprehend the greatness of the day's happenings, the rest were unconcerned. A like condition exists today.

The world-shaking events of that week moved speedily before an awestricken group of disciples. It started with loud voices, saying, "Hosanna to the King," but ere long some were heard to say, "I don't know Him." He was praised, yet blasphemed-they placed their coats and palm leaves before Him, yet they parted His garment among them and cast lots upon His vesture. He had given life, yet they sought to take His. They called Him king, yet treated Him as a criminal.

More and more the pre-written outline of the week's program was being brought to light but I suppose Judas Iscariot had not acquainted himself with it. He stepped as it were upon the stage and began his bargaining to sell his Saviour, just as he was pictured in Zechariah 11:12, 13, hundreds of years before. "And I said unto them, if ye think good, give me my price: and if not, forbear. And the Lord said unto me, Cast it unto the potter: a goodly price that I was prized at of them. And I took the thirty pieces of silver, and cast them to the potter in the house of the Lord."

This betrayer could not have performed more perfectly if he had been practicing for months as if in a play. He was only a part of the activities of this momentous period. Many others participated, the Chief Priest and other religionists, the rulers, the soldiers, the scribes and even the thieves, from the poor to the rich, the lowly and great, they all seemed to get into the stream of public sentiment against Jesus.

Into this the most important week of all ages and for all Christianity, the entire succession of prophecies seem to be poured. This is the time toward which every type and shadow had pointed.

David, the sweet singer of Israel, took pen in hand centuries before this week and by great inspiration gave a clear account of the crucifixion of Jesus. In Psalm 22: 16-18, "For dogs have compassed me: the assembly of the wicked have enclosed me: they pierced my hands and my feet: I may tell all my bones: they look and stare at me. They part my garments among them, and cast lots upon my vesture."

The ridicule and mockery that was heard around the cross on this day of all days revealed that even the most pious religionist had overlooked David's prewritten account of their doings. However, when the sun grew dark and the earth went into a convulsion, and the rocks burst asunder, they were heard to say, "Truly this was the Son of God." If these men would have made an effort to acquaint themselves with the Scripture, they probably could have saved themselves from personal implication. Sadness gripped them as they were faced with the cold fact that they had participated in the death of the Son of God.

They learned the truth too late to help them, as men are so prone to do. No doubt, many were heard to lament over their negligence and say, "If I had taken the time to know the truth, my position would be quite different."

One of the Greatest Revelations of this week was the fact that around one man and the events of one week the entire Scripture was written, without which there would have been no need for such writings. The absolute accuracy of those prewritten accounts gives positive proof that Scripture is the inspired Word of God; which, if you will believe, you will find yourself on sure footing, otherwise you will lament. With those who neglected to know the truth.

The only explanation for the writings of 36 writers who required 1,600 years to compile 66 books which we know as the Scripture, is that each of them was directed by one who knew the beginning and the ending. This mastermind is the Holy Ghost, the third person of the Godhead. He was there at the conference when the great plan of the ages was brought into motion. At proper intervals, part after part, and book after book was added as the Holy Ghost sought out an acceptable man and moved him to write as he was dictated to and inspired. It was logical that these men wrote about things of their day, but the miraculous fact is the way much of their writings resound repeatedly through the ages as many of the symbols become realistic.

Abraham made a thunderous proclamation to his sons, Isaac, on Mt. Moriah, "My Son, God will provide for himself a lamb." He thought he was speaking about an immediate provision but this statement uttered hundreds of years before found its full meaning in Jesus at Calvary.

One by one men of past centuries made prophetical statements about a man whom they knew not, and had not seen, neither would ever see on earth, but the truth of their utterances was revealed when Jesus cried aloud on the cross and said, "It is finished." These glorious facts of the Scripture make it a living word, never an expiration, but always an inspiration.

The Writings of the Prophets about Jesus are like a thousand artists over a period of as many years who, when they passed by, made a stroke with their brush. Nearing the finish some might say, as they observed the painting, "It appears to be a lamb." Others might say, I see it as a priest," while yet another could ask, "Can you not see the emblem of a king?" Each of these observers could have seen the different resemblances because "Jesus was a Lamb, He is the High Priest and shall be King of Kings." We also stand in fulfillment of prophecy spoken by:

"And it shall come to pass afterward, that I will pour out of my spirit upon all flesh; And I will show wonders in the heavens and in the earth, blood, and fire, and pillars of smoke. The sun shall be turned into darkness, and the moon into blood, before the great and the terrible day of the Lord come." (Joel 2:28-31)

"Signs in the sun, and in the moon, and in the stars; and upon the earth of distress nations, with perplexity; the sea and the waves roaring; Men's hearts failing them for fear, and for looking after the things which are coming on the earth: for the powers of heaven shall be shaken. And then shall ye see the Son of man coming in a cloud with power and great glory." (Luke 21:25-27)

Just as surely as the first advent of Jesus came as planned, you may expect Jesus to come again for His Church.

2
Message of the Burning Bush

"And the angel of the Lord appeared unto him in a flame of fire out of the midst of a bush: and he looked, and, behold, the bush burned with fire, and the bush was not consumed."

(Exodus 3:2)

Here a lone shepherd came to the backside of the desert, unto the mountain of God, even Horeb. This was the man who in infancy was hidden in a little ark of bulrushes by the river's brink. His was a miraculous deliverance from the king's decree of death. Moses became a man of decision. In later years he showed his desire to help his Israelite brethren by entering into their personal difficulties, only to be misjudged and as a result fled into the land of Midian. There in exile he was married, and at the birth of his son, Gersham, he said, "I am a stranger in a strange land."

By divine intervention, Moses became the foster grandson of the King, and was thereby heir to royal advantages. But as he lived amid the pomp and splendor of these surroundings, a desire to help his people was constantly present and contentment seemed far removed. It was only human that he should consider his luxurious living with all its natural security. Yet the anguish on the faces of his fellow men stirred the unrest in his heart. This feeling continued to mount higher and higher until one day as a climax he cried, "I choose rather to suffer the afflictions with the people of God than to enjoy the pleasures of sin for a season." He esteemed the reproach of God's people greater riches than the treasures of Egypt.

It was during the time of Moses' wise decision that the Israelite people in Egypt were sighing and groaning by reason of their bondage and they cried unto God and as their cries came before Him, God remembered His covenant with

Abraham, Isaac and Jacob. And God purposed in his heart that he would give them relief. So he set a bush afire in the path of Moses. It burned, yet it was not consumed. It was aflame with the presence of God. There were many bushes in that vicinity, but only one burned. It was a bush of divine calling, not a bush a flicker, but a bush aglow. Many times in the Scripture we have seen fire used to denote God's approval. As with Abraham, when the fire passed through the midst of his sacrifice, at Solomon's temple on the day of dedication when fire came from beneath the altar. On Mt. Carmel when the convincing fire fell in answer to Elijah's prayer. When Isaiah's lips were touched with a coal of fire and he cried, "Here am I, Lord, send me." And in Zechariah's vision of the golden lamp stand where the lamps burned constantly as the oil poured into the lamp stand.

Fire is exciting, powerful and moving. I would that the fire that burned in the bush and called the attention of this traveler was in evidence in all churches throughout America. We can never afford to be reduced to grey ashes of past persuasion. It was this fire that attracted the attention of Moses and caused him to say, "I will now turn aside to see this great sight." It was something extraordinary, spectacular, and different. It was not the bush, dormant and dry, but the bush ablaze with God's glory, that offered the divine call to Moses. When God saw that he had turned aside to see, he called to him and said, "Moses, draw not nigh hither: put off thy shoes from off thy feet, for the place whereon thou standest is holy ground."

Then God identifies himself:

"I am the God of Abraham. It was I that called him out of his tent and asked him to count the stars, which he could not do because they were too many, whereupon I told him so shall thy seed be."

"It was I that sent him forth on his journey, to a land that I would show him." And Abraham went "looking for a city which hath foundations, whose builder and maker is God."

"It was I that put faith in his heart to make him the father of the faithful."

"I am the God of Isaac; it was I that ordered his existence when it was physically impossible."

"It was I that put the ram in the thicket, on Mt. Moriah so that Isaac could go free as he was being offered on the altar of sacrifice."

"I am the God of Jacob; it was I that opened the heavens above Jacob as he lay beside the road."

"It was I who beheld him in his deepest sorrow, and brought him again to Bethel and renewed with him my covenant."

"It was I that smote him on the thigh when he refused to let me go except I bless him."

Realizing he was in the presence of God, Moses hid his face. I believe he felt his own weakness and his personal insignificance. Yet, he no doubt recognized a mighty force of divine unction. He was getting his commission as the leader of God's people and was used mightily by the power of God in the pursuit of his work. The message he received out of the burning bush was a message of deliverance. God said to Moses, "I have surely seen the afflictions of my people."

An affliction is a state of being afflicted. The cause of continued pain of the body or mind, or illness, or losses, it's a grievous distress, misery, calamity or grief. God said, "I have seen it." Nothing occurs that he does not see. He sees the rushing waters of Niagara Falls, and the trickling water of the brooks. He sees the atomic blast, or the lightning bug little light. He sees the giant eagle soaring, or the sparrow falling. He observes the people by the millions, and takes note of one hair that falls. He hears the thunderous storms or the faint sound of the humming bird.

There was not a weeping mother in Egypt, a careworn father, or a whimpering babe, that had escaped his eyes. Not a broken tissue; not a clouded eye; not a heavy ear; not a twisted limb; not a fevered face that had escaped him. He said to them and he says to you, "I have seen your affliction." When you cry out, "Oh God, my heart is broken," He answers, "I have seen it." When you call upon God out of terrible pain, He answers, "I have seen it." As Jesus prayed on the mountain and watched his laboring disciples fight against the tempestuous water to keep their boat afloat, so He is watching his children on their voyage, as they endeavor to combat the storms of life.

His message continued, "I have heard their cry" by reason of their taskmasters. As they cried in their captivity, in bondage and under pressure. I have heard their screams in the night; I have heard their groans in secret places; I have heard their weeping in their rooms; I have heard them sigh as they work.

God heard the wails of a depressed people laboring under the cruelty of an overlord. Sorely vexed by the pain of the lash, and the bruise of their beatings, "I have heard." To be heard by your immediate superior at work, helps you; to be heard by your congressman, pleases you; to be heard by your family, encourages you; to be heard by your doctor, relieves you; to be heard by God delivers you and this is the need of the multitudes across the world.

Many are saying with Job, "Oh that one would hear me: Behold, my desire is that the almighty would answer me." Job must have been in the depths of his despair in this moment, feeling that he was not heard. But faith revived and lifted him to a plateau of courage and he cried out, "I know that my redeemer liveth, and that he shall stand at the latter day upon the earth: and though after my skin worms destroy this body, yet in my flesh shall I see God: whom I shall see for myself, and my eyes shall behold, and not another."

When time has passed by and conditions remain unchanged, and you wonder if relief will ever come, remember the Lord said, "I have heard their cry." "I know their sorrow." The sorrows of which they dare not speak. Of their oppression from which there seems to be no escape. Sorrow to which they have resigned themselves in despair. A nation subdued, held captive, exhausted from strenuous toil. When they cried out to the Lord, He said, "I know your sorrow." I know you are a stranger in a strange land. I know you are slaves to ungrateful masters. I know there is no satisfaction in the fleshpots of Egypt. I know your life has become a dread as you look into a dark future. But, "I am come down to deliver them: to take them out of the hands of the Egyptians, their oppressors." I am come to give them freedom in their own land flowing with milk and honey. I will make them a nation under their own flag.

This deliverance took a miracle to perform. But what is a miracle to God? It is true that it would have looked impossible from a human point of view, but when you remember that everything in existence is an act of God's creation and handiwork, all doubts are dissolved.

God make the Red Sea do a standup act while Israel marched through? He has always controlled the water. He can gather oceans in the palm of His hand if He chooses.

One can almost see Moses standing, trembling, awestricken. The bush still burning and the voice of God sounding forth in deep, resolute tone, vibrating with determination to bless a people who have long since stood in need.

Moses, listening to the message that meant life to his people, realized that every word he received put greater responsibility upon him, yet it seemed that a portion of the flame was being transplanted from the bush to his very life, until by the time the message had ended there stood a lone shepherd burning with holy zeal to run with the message that "freedom and deliverance has come." Being convinced, Moses asked this question, "What shall I say to the people?" They are a multitude of suffering, cringing, subdued people, dying by degrees under the weight of despair. "What shall I say to them?" It may seem too good to be true, and it is possible that they will wonder if such could be. They must be convinced.

"Tell them I Am that I Am." Tell them I Am hath sent you. The Jews asked Jesus, "Thou art not yet fifty years old, and hast thou seen Abraham?" Jesus answered, "Verily, verily, I say unto you, before Abraham was, I am." Before the morning stars sang together, I am. Before Cain grew a garden, I am. Before Enoch built a city, I am. Before Jabal stretched a tent, I am. Before Jubal played a harp or an organ, I am. He, who is "from everlasting to everlasting" has sent you and "I will be with thee."

Pharaoh will not agree to your freedom. The armies will not be at your disposal. Public opinion will turn against you, "But I will be with you." "I will stretch out my hand and

smite Egypt with my wonders and after that he will let you go."
(Exodus 3:20)

When the great arm of the Allies stretched out to the concentration camps of Europe, the troops were heard marching with a steady gait, liberation for captives was at hand. Hearts were made to beat with rapid speed for the joy and ecstasy of being free again. So the stretched out hand of God brings deliverance to every captivated soul who will accept freedom at his hand.

God is a God of deliverance and is awaiting your call. Call out from your hospital bed, or from your confinement at home. In your secret place of prayer or at your work, call out. Wherever you are at this moment, call upon the Lord for the help you need … as we pray together.

3
Double Resting Place

*"Thou art my hiding place and my shield:
I hope in thy word."*

Psalm 119:114

Shunem means "a double resting place"; and if one will follow the events that occur in the lives of two of its people, he will readily see why. This account will help one to leave his fears and desperation. Follow the example of the Shunamite woman and find great relaxation in time of adversity.

> *"And it fell on a day, that Elisha passed to Shunem, where was a great woman; and she constrained him to eat bread."*
> *2 Kings 4:8*

She was an elderly woman, and so was her husband. These two older people lived in an old house. Life was now a matter of routine, an uneventful existence. A kind of dying-by-the-day existence. Their home had lost its laughter. There was no sound of thrills, no hope for future excitement.

However, one day a prophet named Elisah appeared and started his mission with the people of the town. This little old woman was impressed with Elisha and invited him to her house to eat and rest. Seemingly, this was done repeatedly. One day the lady said to her husband, "I perceive that this is a holy man of God . . .. Let us make a little chamber, I pray thee, on the wall; and let us set for him there a bed, and a table, and a stool, and a candlestick: and it shall be, when he cometh to us, that he shall turn in thither" (2 Kings 4:9, 10). The old gentleman agreed. Without knowing it, he had made the greatest decision of his life.

In those days there were no churches and ministers such as we have today. The prophet was God's outlet and contact for the people, so building a room onto their house was equivalent to joining their house to the house of God. Here was God's means of blessing. They were privileged people now with very close contact with God's arrangement. Now Elisha, who had no dwelling place, had been given a resting place. The old couple had a resting place; and now the prophet had one, so it was a double resting place.

It was not expected by the old couple that God would smile upon them for this act. They simply had a desire in their heart to help God's man who had brought the message of hope. Elisha lies on the bed one day and felt that he must make a gesture of gratitude for his newfound place of rest. He asked the lady, "Wouldest thou be spoken for to the king, or to the captain of the host?" She answered, "I dwell among mine own people." To her, building this room was not for reward but a deed from a desire of the heart. Elisha, however hard he tried, could not get the woman off his mind. He asked his servant Gehazi, "What then is to be done for her?" He suggested the fact that she and her husband had no son. Elisah had Gehazi call the woman again. She came to the room of the prophet to get the glad shock of a lifetime. Elisah said, "About this season according to the time of life, thou shalt embrace a son. This of course was impossible to believe. The lady said, "Nay, my lord, thou man of God, do not lie unto thine handmaid."

But God had this couple in mind because of their service of love to His cause. What an example for all of us. If we are meeting problems that seem impossible in our lives, we should strengthen our connections to the cause of Christ, join ourselves harder to the house of God. A pastor recently spoke to me about the policy of one businessman in his church. He said, "When the man's business seems to get a little slow, his giving gets noticeably increased. " This may seem in reverse to good reason, but to me it speaks of partnership with God and faith in God. There is one thing certain: you cannot outdo God, and you cannot do without God.

This account of Elisha's bringing joy to this elderly couple produces such proof. They had received God's message of renewed life. In about a year a cry was heard from the crib. It was a boy, a miracle boy. What an unexpected plateau had been reached by this old couple. New sounds of laughter, hand waving, cries of childhood, and the pitter-patter of little feet brought new life to an old, dying-out home. The couple had found a new resting place something to live for and a new meaning for their existence. They had joined their house to the house of God. This contact with God's man with a message had provided a new way of life.

Their little boy grew and no doubt was like any other child. He had his time of pleasure giving, and then he gave his parents moments of displeasure. He brought upon himself those unhappy occasions of the applying of the rule. This speaks of routine living. They accepted him now as a matter of fact and at times forgot that he was their miracle boy just like many who read the message. You lose sight of the manifold blessings you enjoy, given you only by the hand of God. It has become a daily routine with no special thrill. Life has brought moments of anguish and despair, and you give more thought to those disappointments than to the blessings. This has a tendency toward ingratitude.

One day the little boy went to the threshing floor to visit his father at work. While there he became violently ill. Taken to his mother, he sat on her knees until he died. She did all she could, but he passed away. Now she was to find a rest in her provision of God's house and faith in the word she had received. Rather than fall apart and blame God for this disappointment, she took the little boy in her arms and carried him to the prophet's room. She laid him on the prophet's bed as if to commit the boy into God's hand. It is to be remembered that she only had to go next door. Here was a close association. She had invested in this privilege. She had a right to go in that room and to place her dead boy on that bed as if placing him on the altar.

She went to the threshing floor and asked her husband for a young man and a mule. Her husband asked why she wanted to go to see the prophet. He said that it was neither the Sabbath nor a new moon. How typical of so many today who have to have a set pattern, or rather a rut to follow, in their religious activities; and any extra service is out of the question. She had not told him the news of the son s death, or he too would have gone for the prophet. Here is evidence of a real rest and trust she had found. Where else could one find this consolation and relaxation?

Unlike many of us who question everything and depend upon our own reason and logic, she found a restful trust in God. When this experience came, she had reason to question, "If God did not want me to have this boy, why did he give him to me? I did not ask for a son. It was not my idea. It was a miracle." Now she could have asked, "Why?" But she did not. She told the young man who drove the mule to drive hard and not slack. What courage to be used as a pattern. When impossible adversities come, do not stop and question, why? Drive hard and slack not. She knew her only help would come from the Lord through His servant, as before.

It was no time to depend on routine living or entertain negative thought. She acted as if she expected a reversal of circumstances. Here is the greatest privilege we have as children of God: the privilege of leaning completely upon Him when all other hope has passed us by. To be sure, a usual routine was not sufficient now. It required a resurrection to correct this problem. Yet the life-giving miracle when the boy came, gave grounds and support to her faith for this need. She had been living a life above the ordinary even in her most routine chores ever since she had joined her house hard to the house of God. She had learned that God could do anything and that nothing was out of the realm of possibility. She did not call for a funeral director. She went for an undertaker. Those out-of-reach thoughts are most likely to be evidenced in the lives of those who live out of the realm of natural dependency. It was a sure thing. She would finally bury her boy if she did not first bury herself in complete unswerving faith in God and become unmoved by all things visible.

This place of rest from desperation was in evidence in the answer she gave when one would ask about her husband or her son. She would say, "It is well, or it will be well." Such were the answers when she arrived where Elisha and Gehazi were. However, upon coming to Elisah, the one on whom she was depending and the one who had brought the message of great hope to her, she laid bare her heart. She came to the point of persuasion where her statement and request was to mean life for her son. I like her boldness of speech with the prophet. She said, "Did I desire a son of my lord? Did I not say, do not deceive me?" What a portrayal of declared rights, and she was most definitely acting within her rights. She had furnished the money for that room. She had purchased the bed, and this was the means by which she had been blessed. Her action seemed to say to the prophet, "What are you going to do about it?"

Remember that the Lord said, "Concerning the work of my hands command ye me. It sounds as if she had reached such a position in faith. She had placed her boy on the prophet's hands and had left him to be helped, just as we should bring our burdens to the Lord and leave them. Likewise, we should bring our children and lay them on the altar and expect God to give them life everlasting. Her approach brought immediate response. Elisha gave Gehazi his staff and directed him to go lay it upon the boy. He went and put forth the effort but returned meeting Elisha and the woman with the report that the boy was still dead. This could have added concern to the good lady's mind if she had not concluded in her mind that a resurrection was going to be experienced. The backsets on the way seemed as incidentals. It should be noted here that this was an effort of secondary rank. It was a kind of effort by proxy, which seldom brings the desired result. The only way of success is by absolute personal application to the task at hand. There are some things that can be done by the staff, but such a job as this requires the stretching of one's self. This is what Elisah did; He found the dead boy on his bed, covered with his sheet. This good woman and her husband had purchased both.

Elisah stretched himself upon the boy-eyes upon eyes, nose-to-nose, mouth-to-mouth, hands to hands. Not long after this effort started Elisah began to feel warmth returning to the boy's body. He actually arose from the body, which was showing signs of life. I think he enjoyed the anticipation. It was like a breeze before a rain. Evidence was there, and he wanted to rejoice in the coming victory. I have enjoyed such moments of faith to the extent that it brought a feeling of victory. I have relaxed in the faith prior to the fact. This is the highest type of faith, and it brings into focus the possibility of provision. I think Elisha must have reveled in the knowledge of the impending event. He thought of the excitement of telling the mother that the boy was alive and the expression of her joy upon receiving the news.

These are moments of greatest value, like walking the gangplank to a ship. You are on the approach. It was like the Early Church walking from Christ's ascension to the Upper Room with knowledge that something extraordinary was in the offing. Elisha may have prolonged his waiting for his own enjoyment, but finally he decided that it was time to bring this to a finish, He stretched himself again as before. Radiating the power of God into a body required life. This he did until the little boy sneezed seven times, his eyes opened, his mouth formed a smile, his eyes sparkled, and his complexion grew ruddy. What an accomplishment. What a joy. What a plateau of trust for something seemingly out of the question. My friend, that is where it would have to be, completely out of question and over in the realm of absolute, positive knowledge that God is going to bring about your request.

The little woman was called to the scene of rewarded faith. She was not far away, just next door. When she came in the room and was told to take her boy home now that he was alive, she gave a revelation of the true attitude of her heart. She gave the answer to any question as to why God chose to so bless her. Her action gave pronouncement of her inner gratitude to God. I could not have blamed her if she had run to the bed and grabbed the boy and embraced him out of great joy. This I think most of us would have done. It would have been the natural thing to do. But here is the secret.

She did not do the natural thing. Before she gave vent or expression of her human desire to love her son, she bowed before the man of God and gave thanks to God for His answer to her prayer. It was her attitude toward God that brought her answer. Then she took the little boy by the hand, and together they went home to again enjoy God's miraculous provision.

What a disclosure of God's desire to bless those who enter into His work with sincere heart and absolute truth! This couple could not have invested in anything that offered kind of dividends. The best the commercial world can offer is a return in money, which can beget only more money. This, as enticing as it is, falls short of the dividends offered by the Lord. He offers dividends in the things money cannot buy, plus financial returns.

I think it would pay you who read this message to try God in your problems. If life seems to pass by and your living is uneventful, you should enter into God's arrangement and let Him show you the benefits of a partnership with Him through faith in His Word. Why not join your house hard to the house of God and let God think kindly on your problems. If you have needs, show God that you are going to enter into His work. He will become obligated to solve your problems and answer your prayers. If your children need special attention, God will spread Himself to cover them. Join yourself to the house of God by acceptance of His Word. He offers overall coverage of anyone's desire that abides in Christ and Christ's Word abides in him. This is the promise to anyone who dares to relax in the Word of God.

4

Great Surprise

"For the Lord Himself shall descend from heaven with a shout, with the voice of the archangel, and with the trump of God: and the dead in Christ shall rise first: Then we which are alive and remain shall be caught up together with them in the clouds, to meet the Lord in the air: and so shall we ever be with the Lord."

(I Thessalonians 4:16, 17)

This world is in for a surprise that will throw it into the greatest state of turmoil that could be imagined. When the newscaster and the papers come out with the startling announcement that millions are missing from the earth; when the homes are disrupted by some being taken and some being left; when every baby has been lifted out of every home throughout the world; this will be the shock of all ages for those left behind. But let me hasten to tell you that you do not have to be left. The choice is yours to make, if you make it in time.

If a news commentator were telling you this, he would say it in these words: "A great story is about to break. The world is about to experience something of phenomenal proportions. It is expected that we are about to depart from the usual or customary manner of news and give an account of an experience never before published in any paper.

"The vote-seeking politician, the dictators, the corrupted schemers, the high-headed socialite and the compromising preacher will not be included in this news coverage; but the meek people, the humble people, the unheard of people, as far as the social world is concerned, will be the only subject. They will push every ordinary subject into the shadows as God gives His people their day of rejoicing."

We hear a great deal of sensational announcements in these days as everyone is space-minded. We are kept in suspense as we anticipate the launching of another rocket or satellite. They tell us that the "count-down" has started during which time there is a check for any possible flaw in their equipment.

It reminds me of the account of the death angel that was to pass over Egypt when the first born was to die if blood was not on the door lintel. The zero hour was midnight. The hour continued to come closer and closer to midnight and when it struck, death was experienced in every home that had neglected to prepare. From the palace of Pharaoh to the hut behind the mill there was heard wailing in the wake of this great tragedy.

In Noah's Day, God said to him, "For yet seven days and I will cause it to rain upon the earth." The "count-down" started – 7-6-5-4-3-2-1-0, and the waters began to rise. And the unbelieving people who mocked and laughed at Noah in his preparation for a flood were made to realize that it was no myth.

Today we hasten toward this great event that shall close out this dispensation and bring into being the greatest joy and the greatest sorrow. The rapture of the Church and the leaving of the negligent. It is a sad thing that we are not being more constantly reminded of the nearness of the coming of Jesus. Sadder still is the fact that many have never heard. In either case the result will be the same. If you miss the rapture, you will be ushered into the tribulation, which is a time of trouble such as the world has n ever known. During this time the antichrist will rule and the mark of the beast will be imposed upon men, without which no one can buy or sell. To receive the mark is to seal your doom; to refuse it would mean death by starvation or by the sword.

We have not been left in the dark about the coming of the Lord. The same Bible that promised the first advent of Jesus into the world; that foretold the scattering and regathering of the Jews to their homeland, has given us a clear statement that Jesus is to appear in clouds of glory to gather His people unto Himself in mid-air.

This Book in which these glorious truths are recorded is still the world's best seller, but in most homes it remains unread. This Book that showed the automobile at extreme speed on the broadways before the car was ever in the mind of the inventor, or a concrete road was ever conceived; this Book that shows us blood on the battlefield, the atomic fire and the pillars of smoke from the atomic blast hundreds of years before such energies were known to exist; this Book that was dictated by the Holy Ghost, the third person in the Godhead who was in the conference as the great plan of the ages was brought into motion, records the voice of the angel as he declares to Christ's disciples, "This same Jesus, which is taken up from you into heaven shall so come in like manner as you have seen Him go away." And also it tells us in the words of Jesus, "If I go away I will come again and receive you unto myself, that where I am there ye may be also."

This is the Christian's hope to which he clings in time of stress and strain. When the problems of life weigh him down, he goes on bearing his load with the assurance that it will soon be over. When home life is not the most pleasant, the Christian comforts himself with the fact that there will be a better day. When the diseased body suffers pain that will not cease, and the days drag by like an eternity, there is the consoling knowledge that deliverance has been arranged.

As in the experience of Job after his children had died, flocks, herds, home and all earthly possessions had been taken from him and then his body became more grievously afflicted than any man in history. His wife and friends urged him to give up and die as he sat on the ashes and scraped himself with a potsherd. He had never heard a sermon on the rapture, or that our bodies would be glorified at the coming of the Lord, but out of an inward inspiration he cried, "I know that my Redeemer liveth, and that He shall stand at the latter day upon the earth: and though after my skin worms destroy this body, yet in my flesh shall I see God: whom I shall see for myself, and mine eyes shall behold and not another."

Here Job takes the hand of all fellow sufferers through the ages and bids them look to a time of "blessed hope." A time when every problem will be solved, and every worry has come to and end.

Every dream becomes a reality.

The invisible becomes tangible.

Every faded cheek regains its hue.

Perfect sight returns to every clouded eye.

Every twisted limb becomes straight.

Every shut-in is released from his confinement.

These Are Great Days of Desire.

The president-elect looks forward to Inauguration Day.

The king or queen looks forward to Coronation Day.

The slaves looked forward to Emancipation Day.

The Christian looks forward to Resurrection Day.

Which to God the Father will be the realization of the purpose for which He sent His Son into the world. To the Lord Jesus it will be the joy and glory for which He endured the cross and despised the shame. To the Holy Ghost it will be the end to which He has guided the Church even amidst many hard trials. To the families it will be the greatest family reunion ever gathered together. To the Church it will be the greatest General Assembly of all times, because there will be present the Patriarchs of old, the apostles, the martyrs, the early Church fathers, the Christians of the early Church who, when the glorious gospel burst forth up on the earth, dared to leave their tradition and follow the true light. There will be the heroes of faith and those of these last days who have stood true in the heat of the battle and who stood firm in the face of compromise. Every faithful man from the days of Adam to our present day will be present. They shall come from the north, south, east and west to attend this the greatest of all Christian assemblages.

With the families reunited, and as it were in their pew, I can imagine the great assembly of worshippers beholding the person of our lord and all the notables of every age who have worked to produce such a gathering. They are in for a time of ecstasy such as no mass meeting, however great, could afford.

When Enoch's great-grandson, Jubal, the world's first organ player, sits at the organ; Miriam, the sister of Moses, comes in with her tumbrel; David, the singer of Israel, brings his harp; Solomon's Temple orchestra of the thousands; the choir of thousands of voices together with all the singers and musicians of the ages, all burst forth on the "Hallelujah Chorus" the toils of the road will already have been forgotten, and all the struggles will have disappeared.

As we look about over the multitudes which no man can number, we will see many Christian celebrities of whom we have read so much. Paul the apostle after one of his many battles wouldn't have looked so pleasant, but to see him now, wearing his "crown of righteousness" which the Lord has given him is a joy. Continuing to scan over the multitudes of people you will see many wearing martyr's crowns and recognize them as some you read about. As the joyful occasion proceeds and Isaiah comes into view, he could very well say, "I wrote you about all this," and the apostle Paul could be heard to say, "I told you so."

GREAT SURPRISE

I ask you, people of America and the islands of the sea, "Can you afford to miss the great time known as "The Rapture"?

All this is ushered in at the coming of the Lord Jesus, when He descends from heaven with a shout, with the voice of an archangel and with the trump of God. The thrill in our hearts is that it could occur at any day or moment. I know of no prophecy yet to be fulfilled prior to His appearing. We live in high anticipation.

Yet today our joy is not unmixed, as we realize that our work has brought us in contact with many who have refused to accept the invitation, and for them there awaits everything but joy and ecstasy. I have given a picture of the Christian's future, but there is a corresponding future for those who neglect to accept Christ. While the Church is rejoicing in mid-air with the Lord, those who were not ready to go will undergo the most torturous experiences. The trinity of Hell will be turned loose upon the earth – the devil, the antichrist and the false prophet. During this week of years, which is seven years, peace will be taken from the earth, a great war will result, there will be famine, death by starvation, by sword, and by the beasts, and there will be hailstones of over 100 pounds in weight. Out of the bottomless pit will come a smoke as the smoke of a furnace and the sun will be darkened by reason of the smoke. Out of the smoke will come horse like creatures called locusts, on their heads as it were crowns of gold, and faces as the face of a man, hair as the hair of a woman, and teeth as the teeth of a lion, the sound of their wings as the sound of chariots of many horses running to battle. They will have tails like unto scorpions and there will be stings in their tails; and their power will be to hurt men five months. From this suffering men will seek to die but death will fell from them.

We are speeding toward these events as fast as time can carry us, yet with absolute complacency and unconcern. We see a picture of today's attitude in the parable of the Ten Virgins, who, while awaiting the appearance of the Bridegroom, all slumbered and slept. Some were careless about their oil and their lamps until the Bridegroom came and the cry was made, "Behold the Bridegroom cometh; go ye out to meet him," and they all arose and trimmed their lamps, and those who were ready went in, while the others were left out.

We have been warned that at the coming of Jesus "Two shall be in the field; one shall be taken, and the other left. Two shall be grinding at the mill, one shall be taken, the other left. Two shall be in bed, one shall be taken the other left."

This shows no partiality on Christ's part at His coming, but rather that one has accepted the Lord and the other has rejected Him. The danger in putting off seeking the Lord is the fact that no previous announcement of His coming will be given, other than the signs that are given in the Scripture. These have all been fulfilled and we are playing on borrowed time.

"For as lightning cometh out of the east, and shineth even unto the west; so shall also the coming of the Son of man be."

This is the speed with which the rapture will take place and the Church will be gone. You will have no time to pray or get ready then. If you are not prepared prior to this you are left behind.

When you realize you are left and the seven years of tribulation are facing you, it will be life's darkest moment. When husband looks for his wife and young men look for their parents; when brother and sister look at each other and realize that the rapture has taken place and Dad and Mother are gone, it will be tragic.

You need not think of the church then it will be closed for eternity. Don't look for the pastor; if he was left behind he couldn't help you. Don't call the Sunday School teachers; they will be gone. You need not tune in to your favorite radio preacher; he will be off the air and in mid-air.

But now the opportunity is yours to get ready if you will hurry. But time is running out. Now while you are concerned call upon the Lord and make sure that you will be ready if He should come tonight.

5

Shallow Water

"But when the fourteenth night was come... about midnight the shipmen deemed that they drew near to some country; And sounded, and found it twenty fathoms...they sounded again, and found it fifteen fathoms. Then fearing lest we should have fallen upon rocks, they cast four anchors out of the stern, and wished for the day"

(Acts 27:27-29).

This reading is the account of Paul's voyage to Rome as a prisoner. It was accompanied with contrary winds, dashing waves, and times of darkness. There were many days and nights when the sun, moon, and stars were hidden from view. It beautifully pictures our voyage on life's sea since we embarked on the old Ship of Zion. Not only does the tempest portray our experience, but also we are glad that we can expect a safe landing on the shores of sweet deliverance.

When I read this scripture, I am reminded of a song written by the Reverend R. P. Johnson, "His Breath Is in the Sails." In this song is pictured the launching of a sailboat and the tempest arising to bring great distress and despair; then the last verse gives a joyful finish of the voyage in the following words.

*Look, Pilgrims are landing where angels are standing
on harbors of transparent gold,
The beauties of glory surpass every story that mortal
has dreamed of or told:
What joy and what rapture as heaven we capture by
sailing through stormiest gale.
They feared not the riding for God's hand was guiding,
and His breath was fanning the sails.
Such consolation makes our rough sailing bearable
just to know that God will see us through.*

On this voyage to Rome the storm was so great that the seamen who had battled out many hurricanes were at a loss to know any methods of survival. They had done all that was in their power. But it appeared that their ship would fall apart.

Two weeks is a long time to endure such a fearful experience. It is no wonder that they despaired of their lives. Their appetite had left them, and they refused to eat. Just one glimpse of the sun, or one more view of the moon in her majestic beauty, just a twinkle of a single star would have brought a degree of hope. Nothing spoke of life or hope. This was it. They were finished. Probably in an unguarded moment one could have seen these brawny, muscular men brush away tears of unbearable grief and anguish, feeling that family and home would never bless their sight again.

I know of no one who has completely escaped the dashing waves and contrary winds of the sea of time. Everyone has his share of life's perplexities. Everyone may have different problems, but to him they make up the storms that rock his ship and bring anguish of heart. Occasionally the strongest and most experienced of all will be seen to show signs of weariness of travel.

I am reminded of the trip made by the Christian notables in the ship when Jesus sent them away, telling them to go to the other side while He went to the mountain to pray. They encountered a terrible storm, and it appeared that these apostles and early disciples would surely go into an untimely, watery grave. But Jesus, watching from the lofty place where He prayed, seeing that they could endure no longer, came walking the stormy sea to their rescue. If you recall the account of this trip, you will remember that Peter, when he saw Jesus, cried out and said, "Jesus, if it be you, bid me come to you. Jesus said, "Come." In a moment Peter was walking the waves that had appeared certain to engulf him. What a comforting thought that while we travel here we have the constant care of our Lord who walked the waters and hushed the sea to sleep and caused Peter to walk over the thing that gave him his greatest fright.

This same Jesus sent an angel in the night to visit the Apostle Paul on this storm-beaten bark. This angel spoke to Paul about things that he must do in the future such as appears before Caesar. He knew that if he were to stand before Caesar he could not die here, therefore, he took courage. He came and stood before the frightened crew and said, "Men, be of good cheer. " He had a smile on his face that they had not seen for awhile. No doubt they thought that he had gone mad, that the strain had been too much for him. To talk like this was completely unnatural.

He was not speaking of cheer because the storm had abated- it was still on; not because of a courageous crew-they were despairing, not because of a strong ship-it was falling apart; not because he saw sun, moon, or stars-they were still hidden. He explained, "There stood by me this night the angel of God saying, fear not, Paul; thou must be brought before Caesar. Wherefore, sirs, be of good cheer. For I believe God that it shall be even as it was told me (Acts 27:23-25). Paul was no longer affected by the rock of the ship, the heavy cloud overhead, or the rolling waves. His faith was a sustaining force against these present circumstances.

About midnight the shipmen deemed that they drew near to some country. They listened to the different sounds that indicated a change in depth and position. They had a feeling of an approach being made. What they were approaching they could not tell. It probably gave them a degree of relief.

How often today we hear men of great importance stating that we apparently are coming into a new experience. The world is due for a change. The ministry, but also statesmen, diplomats and rulers are in a state of constant concern over the fearful possibilities that seem to appear on time's horizon. The scientists and technicians of every field are rushing in their efforts, racing against any eventuality. Every intuition tells us that something is in the offing. We of the ministry who specialize in the study of the Scripture feel certain that the next great move will be a spiritual one.

These shipmen measured with a sounding line to determine the depth of water and found the water to be twenty fathoms deep, or one hundred twenty feet. They went a little farther and sounded again to find that they were now in fifteen fathoms, or ninety feet of water. This proved their feelings to be correct: the water was becoming shallow. They were nearing a shore. Leaving the high sea and approaching the shore this spoke of relief from the high waves of the open sea, but the danger now was the rocks along the shoreline.

How this pictures the present voyage of the church. There is no doubt that we are nearing the shore of our promised inheritance, but the rocks of our present position give all who are aware of them a great concern.

Fearing lest they dash against the rocks, they cast out four anchors. It would have been a tragedy to come this far and then hit the rocks so near shore. How typical of today-rocks of confusion, apostasy, complacency, and atheism. Many have traveled almost a lifetime battling every kind of adversity and find themselves on the rocks because they failed to be anchored, as they should.

There are anchors that will hold you, one of which is the Word of God, the divine voice of God to man, the inspired plan and purpose of God for you. Heaven and earth may pass away, but the Word will never pass away. This is the greatest protection against confusion and apostasy. The theories of men may lead you astray, but the Word of God will hold us if we accept it as our anchor.

The love for God and our fellowman constrains us to hold check on ourselves and give us a feeling of obligation. To know that there are those who depend upon us as a faithful, steady Christian whose love and confidence we cannot afford to betray should serve well as an anchor to keep us off the rocks.

Prayer is communion between God and man, and the result of prayer does something to man. It strengthens and assures him. It gives him an attitude of humility. It dissolves doubts and gives clearness of vision. The answer to prayer is like receiving a letter or telegram. It gives assurance of the attention of the sender. Answered prayer denotes the acceptance of the one that is praying. It assures you that the Lord has recognized your faith, and you are rewarded. Hope is a strong anchor. When no inspiration is enjoyed, you hope for it. When feelings do not encourage you, there is hope. When everything goes against you, you continue to hope. When sickness seems to hold you bound, hope for a better day keep you holding on.

Hope is an anchor that will hold you when everything else seems to have failed. Do not turn loose of hope until all other elements of happiness have returned. To lose all hope will guarantee a crash against the rocks. These four anchors-the Word, love, prayer, and hope-will assure you safety against destruction. Never let them go. Be determined to hold your position in God. We are too near the end of the journey to fail now.

When the shipmen had cast out their anchor, they wished for the day. In anticipation they waited. Feeling that land was near and rough traveling was soon to end, they felt a desire for rest and longed for a sign of its coming. Faith had taken hold of Apostle Paul, and he sat down to eat and encouraged all the men to take meat, endeavoring to convince them that their troubles were soon to end.

By our measuring line, the prophecies of the Scripture, we know that the troubles will soon be over for the Christian. We have sounded and have determined that we are now in shallow water, and day-by-day we are drawing nearer to the shore of complete deliverance. There were times when even we can remember that all prophecies were not yet fulfilled. The Jews had not been given their homeland; now they are there. There was a time when we knew nothing of the fire of atomic energy or the pillar of smoke from the blast; but now it has become a common occurrence. There were days when false Christs were never heard of; now you constantly hear of someone's calling himself such. Some of you can remember when there were no chariots with flaming torches on the Broadway, but now the millions are making them. The highways are getting broader just as Nahum prophesied, and there is hardly a moment that an emergency vehicle is not heard from the jostling together of cars on the broadways. Our sounding line shows that we are fast approaching the end of the age.

Second Peter 1:19 speaks of the "sure word of prophecy." These foretold events in the Scripture point out the set schedule and timing of the ages. It is by these prophecies that those who are interested in keeping time with the ages can determine our position in God's arranged schedule. It is only by the Scripture that such knowledge can be gained.

Not only does the Scripture speak of the Israelite nation as a "nation being born in a day," or of the prophecy of automobile, or atomic warfare, but also, and possibly more so, it speaks of the spiritual condition and moral status of the days before the end of the age. The book of Jude, preceding the book of Revelation, predicts the apostasy of the professing church and the low level of sincerity among the ministry. It predicts that they will go in the way of Cain, run greedily after the error of Balaam and perish in the gainsaying of Core. He calls them "spots in your feast of charity... feeding themselves without fear: clouds they are without water, carried about of winds; trees whose fruit withereth, without fruit, twice dead, plucked up by the roots; Raging waves of the sea, foaming out their own shame; wandering stars, to whom is reserved the blackness of darkness for ever" (Jude 11-13).

Jude also quotes Enoch, the seventh from Adam who prophesied of these, saying:

"Behold, the Lord cometh with ten thousands of his saints, To execute judgment upon all, and to convince all that are ungodly among them of all their ungodly deeds which they have ungodly committed, and of all their hard speeches which ungodly sinners have spoken against him. These are murmurers, complainers, walking after their own lusts; and their mouth speaketh great swelling words, having men's persons in admiration because of advantage."

Hopefully, you will read the above scripture slowly and analytically because it is clearly descriptive of this generation and needs very little elaboration. There was never a day when religionists were in such a state of indecision and uncertainty. This added to the tendency toward apostasy, and today deliberate disobedience gives absolute proof of the nearness to Enoch's prediction, "Behold, the Lord cometh".

The Lord explained the moral standards that are to be expected in these days in such a manner as one could expect to read in a daily newspaper of the latest happening. He stated Matthew 24:37, 38, "But as the days of Noah were, so shall also the coming of the Son of man be. For as in the days that were before the flood they were eating and drinking, marrying and giving in marriage, until the day that Noah entered into the ark." We need no one to remind us that our moral standards are just as the Lord pictured here in His comparison. He further indicated that these conditions would prevail at His coming. When you let down your sounding rod to test your position, you find that we are in the closing days of this age.

The latest prophecies that have appeared on time's horizon are the developments in the ecumenical movements among the heads of churches-the strengthening thereby of the Roman Church and the gathering of apostate Christendom into a federation. We watch it develop before our eyes and wonder why men of intelligence make plans for such mergers when their traditions are so far removed one from the other. Yet those who read and understand the prophecies know that it is time that these things will come to pass.

Simultaneous with this spiritual apostasy and ecumenicity is the development of the federation of kingdoms on the geographical setting of the old Roman Empire. This is the United States of Europe, known as the Common Market. The Treaty of Rome brings about this federation. This coincides with the prophecies of the ten kings who will give their power over to the Antichrist and who will rule with him for one hour. Six of these kingdoms are in league today, and the way has been clearing for Great Britain to join which could be the seventh. This shows the preparation for the coming of the Antichrist, but the joy of the Christian is that the real Christ will come first. The apostate church federation will be headed by the false prophet to serve as the religious head during a portion of the Tribulation along with the Anti-Christ. Now are the days of this preparation and time seems to be running out for this dispensation. The prophetic Scriptures serve as the time gauge for the ages.

Jesus gave two promises before He went away. First He said, "And I will pray the Father, and he shall give you another Comforter, that he may abide with you for ever." Second, "If I go and prepare a place for you, I will come again, and receive you unto myself; that where I am, there ye may be also." The Holy Ghost has come, and lives are being blessed. And just as surely Jesus is soon to return, and the Church will realize a glorious landing away from the storms of life.

∼

G. W. Lane served his denomination as Executive in several states and general offices

6

Voice of Calvary

"And Jesus cried with a loud voice, and gave up the ghost."

(Mark 15:37)

The voice of Moses was heard on Mt. Sinai, Elijah spoke on Mt. Carmel, and John the Baptist as the voice of one crying in the wilderness. Every voice had lasting consequence upon the world, yet within the bounds of human faith. From the middle cross atop Mt. Calvary was heard the voice of one who knew no boundaries in time or eternity, in sickness or health, in life or death, in heaven or hell, in heights or depths. At the sound of His voice the heavens did a blackout, the earth went into a convulsion, and rocks were rent until even today rocks and pebbles still show cracks and crevices. This shows the universal power of "The Voice of Calvary."

The absolute necessity of Calvary is recognized in the earliest existence of man and as far back as history is recorded. The disappointment in the Garden of Eden, the disaster of Sodom and Gomorrah, the dissipation of Belshazzar, the doom of Nebuchadnezzar, and the death and destruction in Israel's wars.

The same evil tendencies that brought such havoc to these plunged the entire world into wickedness such as God could not look upon with any degree of allowance, and the earth groaned in its struggle for deliverance. There was none on earth who could meet the need neither a world system nor any man's ability. God and man could not be brought together by the faithfulness of Noah, the loyalty of Abraham, the authority of a Pharaoh, the submission of Joseph or the sweet music of David.

A life must be given- a life without blemish, a life untouched by sin's influence, and whose blood had not been defiled by the venom of sin. If a search were made through the palace of kings, the lineage of all nobility, the aristocracy of the Jews, or the realms of the priesthood, the answer would have been, "As it is written, there is none good, no not one." In the Council Chambers of Heaven it was decided there was only One. God the Father said, "I Will Send My Son."

Jesus coming to the world has been pictured to us from the blood sacrifice of Abel, through the blood sprinkled doors in Egypt, and on the altar of sacrifice of Mt. Moriah, where Isaac inquired of his father Abraham, "Behold the fire and the wood, but where is the lamb for a burnt offering?" Whereupon Abraham answered, "My Son, God will provide Himself a lamb." Immediately a ram was heard rustling in the thicket. As Isaac was saved from death by the provided sacrifice, likewise Jesus became the sacrifice by which the entire world can be made free from eternal death.

Sending Jesus as the Lamb of God into the world was getting ever nearer although unknown to crying humanity, with every passing day and every link in the chain of events, and finally that glorious moment when the angel appeared unto Joseph and said, "And she shall bring forth a son and thou shall call His name Jesus: for He shall save His people from their sins." (Matthew 1:21)

"For This Cause Come I Unto This Hour"

Thus with full realization of His impending death as the main purpose for which He came, He started with His face set as a flint in the direction of the Cross. It is true there would be stops along the way. By no means least among these stops was the Garden of Gethsemane where He took Peter, James and John a little farther with Him. He left the larger body of His followers at the outer edge of the Garden, and then walked alone to a place of communion with God, the Father. It was here that the greater conquest for mankind was begun. It was here where the iniquity of us all was poured upon Him. It was here where He accepted the sickness and diseases of the world so that He could atone for them as He back was beaten with stripes. It is no wonder He cried, "If it be possible, let this cup pass from me." He was fighting the battle of the ages.

The weight of the world was upon Jesus. To add greater grief to His breaking heart, in the heat of the fight were the sleeping disciples, the kiss of betrayal by one of the twelve, and Peter, His most forward friend, lagging behind. In this moment when one friend would have been of the greatest help, they all forsook Him and fled. And alone He is brought before Caiaphas, the High Priest, where the scribes and elders were assembled.

Here before the High Priest, who was chief of the Jewish religion, stood Jesus-ridiculed, accused of blasphemy, spat upon, buffeted, being smitten by the palms of their hands, and being denied by Peter who could not stem the tide of public opinion. Here He was treading the wine press alone.

To Pilate's Hall He Was Led

He stood against the column for His back to be beaten by soldiers who were skilled in the art of scourging. While His back was beaten and bleeding, God said to a sick and suffering world, "and with his stripes we are healed."

They put upon Him the scarlet robe, a crown of thorns was placed upon His head, and a reed in His right hand, representing what they thought of the strength of His kingdom. Bowing before Him they mocked Him saying, "Hail King of the Jews.

Jesus was taken from the judgment hall to be Crucified. As they walked through the streets, they were thronged by the curious eyes from every walk of life. It is reasonable to assume that along the way stood the man whom He had healed of the withered hand, the leper whom He had cleansed, and the blind man with his newly given sight, watching the man who had made it possible for him to see. They could see Jesus struggling beneath the weight of the wood, but their human eyes could not detect the weight of the sins of the world.

As the procession passed through the city gate and winded their way up the hill they may have seen the tree which served as a gallows to take the life of Judas, who sold his Savior and could find no place of repentance. With determined gait the procession drew nearer to the place of the skull . . . Jesus, carrying the cross which was the most shameful means of death, struggled beneath His load. His human strength could no longer endure and His knees buckled. It was not for fear, neither out of indecision. His purpose was stronger than death. We have no record of the weight of the cross causing any other to become exhausted; therefore, we conclude that the weight of the world was the reason for His strength failing. His cross being given to another.

They Came to the Place Called Calvary, the battle-ground where the greatest conquest recorded in the annals of history was about to be waged. It was not a war of nations, but a battle between the "prince of the power of the air" and the Prince of Peace. A battle for complete victory for the forces of righteousness, where the "bruised heel of humanity" was about to strike the head of the serpent.

Standing there was the soldier who was there as a matter of duty, maybe not by choice, yet he was guilty; the chief priest, a traditional religionist actually joining the fight mocking with the scribes and elders; the centurion, who was in charge of the soldiers carrying out the orders of the crucifixion, no doubt feeling his importance ; the passer-by, who was not especially interested and really too busy to stop; the bystander, some greatly concerned, some just watching, some curious ; the daughters of Jerusalem, who stood weeping out of real love and sympathy.

In the midst of all these stood one trembling with human exhaustion, pale from loss of blood, patches of beard missing from His face, His hair matted with blood from His thorn-pierced head. The fight was on, and He was receiving His battle scars. He is the one on whom, as a scapegoat they had laid their sinful hands. . . . He is the sin offering about to be sacrificed for all humanity. He was bearing in His body the sins of us all.

The Moment Has Come

Heaven's sacrifice for the sins of the world is laid upon the Cross. His hands were fastened to the cross with one sling of the sledge. The Hands that tossed out racing planets and a blazing sun; set the stars in their position; lifted little children into His arms; laid a blessing upon their heads; had touched and healed the deaf ear, the blind eye, and sick bodies; brushed away all tears from weeping eyes; soothed the fevered brow.

These hands were now stretched, tearing and bleeding in sight of some He had blessed, yet the pain in these hands was nothing to compare with the severe pain that must have been in His heart. Standing there amid the scoffing, mocking and ridicule his purpose was unaffected by the attitude of the mob. His was a fight to the finish.

There were wagging heads, doubting minds, babbling tongues, rattling dice and the calling of the gamblers' play as they cast lots for his garments. His followers seeing the apparent victory of His enemies, may have found it hard to fight off the feeling of defeat. As they watched Him grow steadily weaker with every passing moment, a feeling of despair gripped their hearts. They felt that this was the end of all their hopes. Scepticism was rank, contrary opinions were openly expressed. The multitudes milled and religionists grew bolder in their claims. The air was filled with nothing but doubt the people seemed unmoved.

But Wait, nature has something to say. Old Man Sun, when he saw the drops of blood, then closed his eyes and refused to shine. Old Mother Earth who had withstood great fallings of water, burst of volcanoes, the heat of the sun, the storm of the ocean, the rise and fall of great kingdoms when she felt the blood of her Creator fall on her back, trembled and shook like a tree in a hurricane. And finally it shook loose the chains of death, hell and the grave, and brought redemption to the soul of fallen man ; something that 96 elements of the earth, stacked as high as the heavens and set off with spontaneous explosion could not do.

During this three hours of darkness and the convulsion of the earth, together with the rocks breaking asunder, the attitude the of people around Calvary underwent a great change. They were heard to say, "Truly this was the Son of God."

The soldiers stood in fear, the religionist ceased to brag, the Christian's hopes revived, and a voice was heard from a thief on the cross, "Master, when thou comest into thy kingdom, remember me." And Jesus, while in the jaws of death gave life another. He had submitted Himself to the Cross, their suffered ridicule, refused the vinegar and gall and gave life to a dying thief. After this He said,

"It Is Finished"

The soldier passed the word to the Sanhedrin, He said "It is finished." The priest passed the word to the scribes and elders, "It is finished." The scribes and elders passed the word to the Pharisee, "He said, 'It is finished.'" To the shepherds and doorkeepers the word passed, "It is finished." To the sick and suffering in the hospital the word passed, "It is finished." To the dead in the graves is passed the word, "It is finished."

To the man bound by sinful habits is passed the word, "It is finished."

The Voice From Calvary though spoken in the whisper of a dying man, has been amplified by its purpose into a thunderous tone, that reached into all ages past, present and future, time and eternity.

The cry for a sacrifice from the Garden of Eden is answered, "It is finished." The demands for righteousness from Sinai is answered, "It is finished." The request of the dying thief for remembrance is granted, "It is finished." The cry from the invalid is answered, "It is finished." The confession of sin by the penitent is answered… "It is finished."

**Speaking through an interpretor
World Conference in Korea**

7
Perfect Law of Liberty

"But whoso looketh into the perfect law of liberty, and continueth therein, he being not a forgetful hearer, but a doer of the work, this man shall be blessed in his deed"

(James 1:25).

When law is mentioned, many will readily think that one is going to deal with restrictions or limitations; but to draw that conclusion about this subject would be entirely erroneous. The law of liberty is exactly what the subject implies, a law that guarantees freedom. It is actually a law to which God binds Himself, the substance of which would like going this, "If my people are willing to meet my requirements, I will meet their needs." These words so arranged are not found in the Scripture, but they are the description of the combined promises of God. Jesus said in John 15:7, "If ye abide in me, and my words abide in you, ye shall ask what ye will, and it shall be done unto you." Again He said in Luke 11:9,10, "Ask, and it shall be given you; seek, and ye shall find; knock, and it shall be opened unto you. For every one that asketh receiveth, and he that seeketh findeth, and to him that knocketh it shall be opened." God guarantees His blessings to us on the grounds that certain conditions are met.

You do not have to worry about God performing His part of the agreement. His part has already been arranged. He is waiting on us. God is not slipshod and does not do business on a hit-or-miss basis. He binds Himself by covenant to His creation and leaves nothing to doubt or question.

God gave His covenant to us not only by oral and written statement but also by chosen and anointed men. He handed down to us a copy of His perfect law, which is for us, and unto Him. This covenant is the Bible, which has been sealed by the blood of Jesus Christ, the Testator. There was never a document bound by a greater seal. When you deal in real estate or the sale or purchase of anything you relax and become perfectly at ease after the legal documents are signed because you are both bound by law to live up to the written agreement. God was so mindful of us that He gave His covenant to us in a manner that we could review it as often as we will. He has no purpose but to carry out every pledge He made. There is no reason why we cannot relax in complete trust in God. God's laws to Himself are yea and Amen, and not one has ever been broken. When there has been a change of plans, He has made it known perfectly to all men.

The Constitution of the United States, by which, and around which, all other laws are formed, can be changed by the proper vote. Our national and state laws can be and are changed. We are not assured that any law will stand if it is determined by the vote of men. It is most gratifying to know that we do have something that holds steady and cannot be changed by the will of the people. We can hold to God's promises as a great anchor.

The provisions of the Law of Moses were weak and could not do a complete work for the people, so it was removed. It was weak because it had an inferior sacrifice. The blood of bulls and goats could not suffice for mankind because they were inferior creatures. These sacrifices served as the strength of the law's underwriting, and the guarantee was weak. Nothing is any stronger than its guarantee or underwriting. So, as stated in Hebrews 10: 9, "He taketh away the first, that he

Perfect Law of Liberty

may establish the second." And in Hebrews 7:22, "By so much was Jesus made a surety [or guarantee] of a better testament." The new covenant, or New Testament, is the perfect law of liberty; and it is established. This New Testament is not in existence by vote or human sanction but by Jesus standing in judgment before accusers and taking the brutal beating, and then the total all-out gift of Himself on the Cross. He paid the price for everything offered to mankind by God the Father. The Covenant is irrevocably established.

God's established laws that we depend upon every day have never failed. We trust in God's plan unconsciously every day of our lives. If God is true to one promise, why not trust Him with all the promises He has made? He established the law for the sea when the earth was completely covered with water. God called the water into separate bodies of water and called them seas. In this way the earth came forth to the surface and was made productive. Today we live as far away, or as close to, the water's edge as we choose and feel safe behind God's great floodwall. This floodwall is neither visible nor manmade. It is an established law for the sea that says, "Stay in your place"; and the sea cannot climb over God's law.

The vast population in Florida, the Carolinas, Georgia and the other coastal states may not have given it much thought; but if it were not for God's law that holds the Atlantic back, they would be moving, or already gone. But they accept God's care for them and have no worry. This is an established law for their liberty. They watch the tide come in and watch it go out, but they live relaxed. They know the schedule of its movement and rest in the established law for the water. Many times one hears it said, "Old Mother Nature sure knows her business." This is not governed by the knowledge of Mother Nature, but by the arrangement of Father God.

"And God made two great lights; the greater light to rule the day, and the lesser light to rule the night. He made the stars also." God arranged for the sun, the greater light to produce light for the day and also to reflect light on the moon at night. The moon cannot shine of itself but is dependent upon the sun. It is occasionally seen in the day, but scarcely noticed. God's law for the solar system shows His ability to keep order in His arrangements. If He were not a God of precision and absolute order, and was as loose as we are at times, there would be all kinds of accidents among the stars; they would be falling everywhere. But we have no fear of such incidents. When we see a star getting out of place, it streaks through the elements with a flash and falls into fragments never to be seen again. What God establishes remains entirely in accordance to His will? God has arranged for day and night as one of His universal laws, and there is no slip up in its execution. He did not say that the sun would give light only in the day, but He said that it would rule the day.

With or without the knowledge or consent of the inhabitants of the earth, we are ruled by it – the believer, unbeliever, skeptic or atheist, all alike. Whatever we do is done in keeping with the activities of the sun. We retire and get up by the sun. We go to work and go home by the sun. We set all appointments by the sun. Though one may claim to be an infidel and try to get along without God, yet he has to respect His established laws if he keeps in step with the world's activities. This has been true ever since Creation. Without the sun's rule of the day, there would be no set time of the day or night. The time clock would mean nothing. The different time zones are set in keeping with the sun. The sun governs winter and summer so that we plan and reap by the sun. One may not honor all of God's laws, but this is one with which he keeps in step.

The Lord Jesus gives a beautiful picture of the church when He said, "I am the light of the World"; and in turn He said, "Ye are the light of the World." We cannot give light of ourselves; but just as the moon reflects the light of the sun, we reflect the light of the Son of God. In accordance to the position of the moon in relationship to the sun, it is at established times a full moon; if it is slightly to the side, it becomes a three-quarter moon; or a half moon, then a quarter moon. When it is altogether out of range, it gives no light. There are times when it goes into total eclipse. Jesus said, "Without me ye can do nothing." When we are aware that we are in a spiritual eclipse, it is comforting to know that we can get back into proper range so that our light will shine again. God has no desire to be hidden from you, but He has established His position so that you will know how to find Him. If at any time you find that you are out of range of the sun, get back into position so you, like the moon, can reflect the glory of the Saviour: you can take of the suffering, death, resurrection, and ascension and shine it on palace and dungeon, on heathenism and skepticism and bring light of hope to those who sit in darkness and despondence.

One has said that when such light is given forth, it makes the maple appear as silver and the lakes as shining mirrors; the cliffs lose their ruggedness, and the poor underprivileged man thanks the Lord for giving him a ray of light in the window of his hut. This is the beauty of God's arrangement for the benefit of mankind. Can any man say he does not appreciate the laws of God? Some years ago as I traveled I listened to car my radio and heard a very interesting occurrence. I heard Mr. Lowell Thomas say, "In a given number of seconds summer will be officially here." He was in a planetarium where a device had been arranged so that the sunrays would set off a whistle to signify the exact moment. At ten seconds he began the countdown. The whistle sounded and Mr. Thomas said, "summer is here." summer and winter come as God's arrangement dictates. God's work is precise, and very much unlike some would have us believe that "anything goes." Some are like the farmer who walked to the end of the row in his field one morning and pulled out his watch and said as he looked at the sun, "Old Sol is early this morning. " He seemed to think that the sun would come and go according to his watch; but not so, for we will have to set our watch with the sun.

I like to think of the most official timekeeping by which our railroads, airlines, broadcasts and everything that has to

Perfect Law of Liberty

be accurate are regulated – the "Naval Observatory Time." This sign is seen very often under the clock. This sign means that this clock is connected with the big master clock, which keeps it up with the time. The master clock is regulated every hour on the hour according to the sun and moon. When the master clock is regulated, it automatically sets every clock that is connected with it, Very often you might be looking at one of these clocks and see it skip a minute or two and think that something is wrong with it. But not so, the old master clock just pulled it into line and said, "Catch up. A bellboy in a Mississippi Hotel said about their clock, "That thing hums every hour on the hour. " What a good thought he presented. If every one could be so connected with his Master that he would "hum" every hour on the hour, it would be a great thing. All of this is included in the law of God which says that the "Sun shall rule the day." It proves beyond any shadow of a doubt that God's laws are infallible. You can depend on God, and in this trust you can have peace of heart and soul.

The Pool of Bethesda was a body of water that was seasonally touched by the angel of the Lord. At this time when the water was troubled, the first one who entered the pool was made well of his disease. The nature of trouble mattered not. It was a cure-all. This was not a natural provision, but God established this by His mercy as a place where people could find help. Many went there sick and suffering and went home well. As these people came to the pool and waited for the moving of the water, they had no doubt about its power to heal them. Their faith in the benefits of the pool were unwavering. When they saw a man go into the water, they knew he was on his way home. They did not think of failure. The foundation of their faith was the law of God that arranged it. It was great; yet for all the help it gave men, it was limited. Only one could be helped at a time. It was only seasonal, not constant in its operation.

Jesus came that way on one occasion, and there he saw the multitudes as they lay around the pool. The impotent, blind, halt, withered and infirm were there. He saw a man who had been there thirty-eight years who had an infirmity. Jesus had compassion on him, as he knew he had been there a long time and asked him, "Wilt thou be made whole?" He answered Jesus, "Sir, I have no man, when the water is troubled, to put me into the pool: but while I am coming, another steppeth down before me." Here Jesus saw an opportunity to show to the world His plan of bypassing anything that was only a partial help. When this man complained about having no one to help him, Jesus said, "Rise, take up thy bed, and walk." When Jesus found him, he had his back on the bed. When He left him, he had his bed on his back going up God's bypass. Jesus took the place of the limited pool with its seasonal blessing. He took the place of any man who might have been expected to help and showed to the world His plan that all benefits are to be expected through Jesus, the Son of God.

Through Jesus there is a fountain opened in the House of David for sin and uncleanness. It is perpetual in its offer to as many as will call upon His name. The way to become a recipient of God's plan of grace through Christ is simple. Do these three things: (1) forsake your sins, (2) confess your sins to God, and (3) believe God to forgive your sins. Peace will flood your soul, and by His stripes you can be healed.

> *"For ever, O Lord, thy word is settled in heaven"*
> *Psalm 119:89*

8
Altar to the Unknown God

"For as I passed by, and beheld your devotions, I found an altar with this inscription, TO THE UNKNOWN GOD. Whom therefore ye ignorantly worship, him declare I unto you,"

Acts 17:23.

The great Apostle Paul found himself alone in this great heathen city of Athens, Greece. He may have come in unnoticed at first, but with or without their knowledge, there was a human dynamo in their midst, one whom to watch is to be inspired. He carried such a charge of God's presence with him that one way or another he made an impression with everyone he met. He was completely convinced of his Christian doctrine. He never showed any inclination to waver, to question his belief, or to be afraid of any contradiction. His contention was, "If our gospel be hid, it is hid to them that are lost." This was not born of criticism but of compassion, and was a definite call to action when he was confronted with a condition that needed correction. Winning souls was his business; many times they had to be convinced before conversion, but he did not draw back from the task. He seemed to make a habit of taking hold of a problem according to necessity. There is no doubt that he saw a real need in Athens as soon as he arrived.

He was not there as a member of a group. He was not attending a church convention. He stood out as an individualist who was not a part of the city's activities. He stood alone. Like his Master when His followers forsook him, he affirmed that his Father was with him. Paul was alone, but his attitude appeared to be as one who declared he was never less alone than when he was alone. Paul was alone, but accompanied by his convictions; alone, but supported by his compassion, anointed by the third Person of the Godhead, and strengthened by his memories of past victories

Paul did not require the fanfare or drum beating of the bandwagon to inspire him into action. Just the knowledge of multitudes lost and groping in darkness was enough to set him in motion. To observe these people in their dignity and cultural attainment one might think they were so mature in their thinking that they had no need, but that was not the standard by which need is gauged. Then, as now, many who are rich in culture and worldly attainments are destitute of spiritual blessings. They are at the top in popularity, worldly wisdom and wealth, but at the bottom in the knowledge of godliness.

Athens was the seat of much that was to be desired. It was here that the form of humanity was portrayed in its greatest beauty. It was in this city that human eloquence attained its utmost heights. This, however, did not affect the great apostle's persuasion of the error in the Athenians' religious practices. All too many miss the simplicity of God's plan in their efforts to make religion a thing of beauty and a ritual of grandeur. Actually, it has always been a militant plan of warfare against evil and has fought its battles with suffering and bloodshed. Everyone who desires its benefits is invited to carry His cross.

Paul saw no signs of this humility in their worship, although he was impressed with their much devotion. He noticed their occupation with religion as he walked through the streets of the city into the heart of its commercial and social activities.

Altar to the Unknown God

This center was known as the marketplace. Here the people met for their shopping and to hear celebrities speak. Here they exchanged any new thoughts and advice that they had gathered.

Paul lost no time. He took advantage of the milling multitudes in the marketplace; also in the synagogue he disputed with their philosophers. They did not know who their guest was. They knew nothing of his connections. Some called him a babbler. Others said, "He seems to be a setter forth of strange gods." This they concluded because he told them of Jesus and His resurrection. It is strange that such an accusation would come from a city with so much religious thought, but Paul had a message entirely different to those usually heard. There is, however, one thing Paul was never accused of cowardice. I believe he enjoyed a challenge.

Here was a condition unequalled anywhere unless it had been Babylon, which was known as the "land of graven images." In Athens the people were entirely given over to idolatry. One could hardly stand anywhere in Athens without seeing temples and statues of gods in great numbers. Some have said it was less trouble to find a god than a man. Some of the streets were so crowded with sellers of idols that it was hard to pass. These people had erected altars to everything and anything. Altars were there in honor of fame, modesty, energy, and persuasion and for fear of pity leaving out or ignoring a god they erected an altar "To the Unknown God."

All this was too much for the great apostle; he could not be quiet. His conversation was so different he attracted their attention and aroused their interest in a great way. He set himself for the defense of the gospel and put himself wholly to the task. He caused no small stir. The people brought Paul to Aeropause, or Mars' hill, which was parallel to the Sanhedrin court. It was the highest court in that land. They inquired of him saying, "May we know of this new doctrine? For you bring certain things to our ears. We would like to know what these things mean." What an opportunity to give release to his feeling!

Then Paul stood in the midst of Mars' hill or the high tribunal. Probably he was too stirred to remain seated, He had a message that was burning his very soul, and he was glad to deliver it. I am sure every minister knows exactly how Paul felt. He came straight to the point and poured forth his soul. "For as I passed by, and beheld your devotions, I found an altar with this inscription, TO THE UNKNOWN GOD. Whom therefore ye ignorantly worship, him declare I unto you."

From there he proceeded to preach to them about the God whom he knew. He told them that God had made the world and all things therein, that He was God of heaven and earth and could not be contained in their temples made with hands. "Neither is worshipped with men's hands, as though he needed anything, seeing he giveth to all life, and breath, and all things. For in him we live, and move, and have our being" (Acts 17:22-28). The Godhead is not like unto gold, or silver, or

Altar to the Unknown God

stone, graven by art and man's device. He preached to them of the worship of repentance, righteousness and the Resurrection. Just as is the case today, some of his hearers mocked at his doctrine; others desired to hear more and certain men clave unto him and believed.

His audience was made up of people who worshipped at different altars. Some worshipped at the altar of fame, energy, altar pity or modesty. Some lingered around the "To the Unknown God." He gave them all alike the one gospel and the only gospel that He could help them. He presented to them the one true God so they would no longer be ignorant of Him.

Paul was well able to represent Christ, had because He been introduced to him in a remarkable way. While journeyed toward Damascus to persecute Christians he met Jesus, who served as the evangelist in his conversion. Jesus was not an easy-going evangelist; He knocked him to the ground and smote him with blindness and made him a submissive soul. What an introduction! He was in position to say, "Him declare I unto you. Paul, being arrested on this Damascus Road, cried, "Who art thou, Lord!" The answer came back, "I am Jesus whom thou persecutes."

During those three days of blindness while fasting, and praying he had a real opportunity to become acquainted with the Lord. Paul was taught the doctrine and given an understanding of things to come by the "Lord of glory." God gave him his commission to preach and serve as His ambassador in many fields, and Paul enjoyed the endowment of power to accomplish his task. When one in his efforts to convert a soul hindered him, he turned to the man interfering and said, "You shall be blind for a season," and they had to lead him away. When the demon-possessed girl troubled him, he rebuked the demons and set her free. When he was put in jail he sang and praised God until the jail had a crack-up and the jailor and his family were saved.

His contact with God was not just a theory or knowledge acquired by reading, but a personal touch from God which was greatly in evidence in his life. It was no wonder that he said, "Him declare I unto you." Too many people know God just as most of us know our governor or president. We vote for him, we read about him, we see his picture, and we respect his official position, but we have never had the opportunity to get personally acquainted.

It is possible to become truly acquainted with God. You can talk to Him; you can feel His presence. You can ask Him for your needs and get an answer just like receiving a telegram from home. He invites us to draw nigh unto Him, and He will draw nigh unto us, Know Him as your heavenly Father who longs to supply every need, and who has arranged for happiness. Paul declared Him as the source of peace to the troubled soul, as the fountain of that would make life worth living for the despondent, the healer of all manner of diseases for the sick and suffering, and the resurrection and the life for every child of God.

What a joy it is to see men became acquainted with the Lord! In recent months I have been afforded a great thrill as I have seen men and women whose lives were so uneventful, lived only to work and come home to drink and eat and carry on in the same routine for a lifetime, when they found God and the sun began to shine through their lives became worth living. It gives a minister a real urge to declare Christ to the world. He is everything you need, and He is the answer to your every problem. You need to become acquainted with Him.

The altar is not a stone set up as a mark of memories; neither is it a shrine erected to honor a god that used to be. The altar is a place designated to meet God and to Him as one you know as your God. Let should be the most sacred place to the Christian because it is the place of communion with God. It should be the most longed for place to the sinner for there he can unburden his soul to God who will lift his load and carry his sorrows, It should be the place most hungered-after for the wanderer, for there alone can he have the assurance that he is at home again.

The altar is the very heart of Christian worship and should never be forgotten. This altar does not have to be erected in any certain place; the beauty of the Christian's privilege is that he can make an altar anywhere. I am not given to the practice of looking back because I think we are living in the greatest day that has ever been, but there is one thing I think about in yesteryear that we should follow very earnestly - the fervent effectual praying to God as One we are close to, and know well.

My mother, who went to be with Jesus a few years ago, had an old, oval-top metal trunk at our house in Texas where she knelt to talk to God. Very often I would hear her praying even before I entered the house as I came from school. My father would have prayer with the family and then permit us to retire, but he spent many nights in prayer, I would awake to hear his low whisper to the Lord whom he knew well as the God who answers prayers, this is the answer to your desire for close fellowship with God.

We remember the patriarchs who lived around the altar and were greatly used of God in their day, Noah found favor in God's sight and built the ark for the salvation of those who would accept in his day; he knew God as a mighty deliverer. After riding the waves of the flood he came out of the ark and built an altar to God, and God put a rainbow in the cloud, Abraham built an altar on Mount Moriah to offer Isaac to God, and Gad gave him a ram in the thicket as a substitute.

After great disappointment with his family, his daughter disgraced, and his son's murderers, Jacob was instructed by the Lord to return to Bethel and build an altar, which he did. God renewed His covenant with him and called him Israel, which means "Prince of God." Elijah, meeting a great challenge by the prophets of Baal, had agreed that the God who answered by fire would be their God. The Baal worshippers spent much time and went through much effort, but Baal did not answer. When they had finished Elijah rebuilt the altar; without fear or doubt he called upon God in a very short prayer and the tire fell. He prayed to God whom he knew, The Baal worshippers acknowledged, and "The Lord he is God." It is great to get a direct answer from God.

The altar is one of the most important things of any man's life, No life can be properly arranged unless it is built around the altar. The different segments of your living depend largely upon the altar without which nothing will fall into place, Make one by the side of your bed, in the barn, in the field, or wherever you are at this moment. Make you an altar and tell God you want to become acquainted with Him, and He will meet you.

9
Forgotten Prophecy

*"Rejoice greatly, O daughter of Zion;
shout, O daughter Jerusalem:
behold, thy King cometh unto thee:
he is just, and having salvation, lowly,
and riding upon an ass, and upon a colt
of the foal of an ass,"*

Zechariah 9:9

Four hundred and eighty-seven years before Christ came into the world this prophecy was written. It may have seemed of little importance how He should ride into Jerusalem, and it could have been easy for this utterance to fade out of their minds. Many had no knowledge of such a prophecy. Only the scholars of the Scriptures would have known it because it was written almost five centuries before. However, those who had the knowledge had forgotten. Not until they saw the prophecy fulfilled before their eyes was it brought to their remembrance, as we read in John 12:12, "Then remembered they that these things were written of him, and that they had done these things unto him."

The tendency of men to forget is a dangerous one. We are too forgetful. If men could bear in mind the words of God, their experience with the Lord would be richer, human failures would be fewer, and churches would be fuller. The forgetfulness of mankind has caused many to neglect their soul salvation.

It was a real vision of God's purpose and plan that made our decision so definite at the beginning, but it is the faded vision that causes the extreme carelessness of this late Christian hour. It is the same-clouded memory that makes it easy to yield to temptation and astray. This is the reason some of our friends are backslidden. They failed to remember the words of God.

Here is one thing that must be remembered, God does not forget one of His prophecies. They will all come to pass. How minutely God carries out His plan is shown in the fact that Jesus did not ride a carriage; neither did He ride a camel into Jerusalem. As it was written, He rode into Jerusalem on an ass.

Does it seem strange to you that on this given day the farmer staked the little ass at this particular place! Does it appear strange that Jesus knew where to send for the little colt! God shows the world through this incident that He will operate His schedule as planned through people who know nothing of the plan. Our God is a God of precision. There is nothing slipshod or wishy-washy about God, and if we plan to have any part with Him we shall have to keep step with His schedule.

"Then remembered they when they saw Him riding on the ass before them. There was no tragic memory in connection with this occasion, but when the prophecies are fulfilled that have been spoken for our day, some of them will be tragic. You may be assured that everything on God's calendar will come to pass just as it is scheduled.

David, the sweet singer of Israel, lived hundreds of years before Christ came into the world. He was a writer of songs. It is possible that he just wrote them as a matter of personal pleasure or personal worship. It is doubtful that he had any idea that he was writing prophecy that would describe world-shaking events that would shape the destiny of millions. His Psalms described the crucifixion of the Lord Jesus in minute detail hundreds of years before it took place. In Psalm 22 we find written, "For dogs have compassed me: the assembly of the wicked have enclosed me: they pierced hands and my feet. I may tell all my bones: they look and stare upon me. They part my garments among them, and cast lots upon my vesture" (Psalm 22:16-18). David had no way of knowing of the event of Christ's death, but God guided his thinking and held his pen so that such a prophetical utterance could be made.

The people of Christ's generation on the earth could have read this, and some could have spared themselves of personal implication in His death if they had bothered themselves to know. The religionist of His day probably had read David's words many times but had forgotten, and while the sun was staging a blackout, the earth shaking and rocks breaking, the people who before had let it slip their minds cried out, "Surely this was the Son of God." It was too late now as they saw the fulfillment before their eyes. They had crucified Him just as the Psalmist said they would. They pierced His hands and feet and gambled over His vesture.

David had made another prophetical statement that showed our God to be a God of precision when he said, "He kept an of his bones, and not one of them is broken." It was a custom to break the legs of those being crucified that they might die more rapidly; this they did to the two being crucified along with Jesus, but when they came to Jesus, He was already dead. It would not have mattered physically to have His bones broken, but God gave the world one more lesson in His absolute planning. God is careful in small things as well as great, and there are no slip-ups with God. Time does not erase His memory.

The Bible that you and I love so dearly is the most up to date book in existence. There are some books just off the press. There are newspapers printed today, and newscasters who have spoken in the last few moments, but the Book of which I speak is more current in its content than the latest newscast. They tell you what has already happened, but the Bible tells you tomorrow's news, and the news for the next thousand years.

It is said that some of the more experienced men in news prediction are eighty-three percent accurate in their predictions. I would think that is very good. This would require a lot of analyzing of world conditions and possibilities. However, I have a Book here that is one hundred percent accurate and through the years has never missed a single prediction, neither in the events nor in its timing. If you care to study this Book you need not be caught unaware of any of God's schedule. Too many are like the old gentleman who stepped to the end of the row on his farm, pulled out his watch and said to him, "Old Sol is coming up early today." He thought the sun should rise by his time, rather than setting his watch by the sun.

We stand in fulfillment of prophecy in our day. "The husbandman waited patiently for the precious fruit of the earth, for the former and the latter rain." The early church beginning at the day of Pentecost enjoyed the former rain.

About the turn of the century the latter rain began and we are enjoying it today. Great spiritual awakenings have been realized. Many are receiving the baptism of the Holy Spirit. Great revivals are being experienced. Recognition of the Pentecostal experience is being shown by many whom at one time questioned it. Today there is no need for anyone to be lacking in his spiritual life if he will give heed to the admonition of Zechariah, who said in Zechariah 10:1, "Ask of the Lord rain in the time of the latter rain; so the Lord shall make bright clouds, and give them showers of rain, to every one grass in the field."

It is the Lord's good pleasure to give every individual the help he needs during this great outpouring. Many have overlooked or forgotten that this great experience is ours today.

God has not left us in the dark about today's events. In Joel 2:28, 29 He has told us of this spiritual outpouring. He said, "And it shall come to pass afterward, that I will pour out my spirit upon and all flesh; your sons and your daughters shall prophesy, your old men shall dream dreams, your young men shall see visions: and also upon the servants and upon the handmaids in those days will I pour out my spirit." It was this Scripture that Peter quoted on the Day of Pentecost when he preached the great sermon explaining the happenings of the day.

Along with this spiritual blessing, God has given us a preview of other things of another nature that will occur. Joel

2:30, "And I will show wonders in the heavens and in the earth, blood, and fire, and pillars of smoke." Joel spoke of these happenings long before the actual events, but you are witnessing them in your lifetime. The most talked about issues of the day are centering upon these events. Blood has flowed and is flowing in the conflicts of our time. Wars have been, and more wars are talked about. The more recent years have brought into action the most devastating fire ever known to man. Joel was not talking about forest fires or home fires; he was speaking of a fire that would be of world-wide concern, that would affect the peoples of the whole world-fire that renders the earth barren I speak of the fire produced by the atmospheric energies, atomic and hydrogen.

The pillars of smoke were a term entirely lost to the human, thought until the most recent years. We had seen smoke rings, puffs of smoke, and smoke rolling from huge engines. But a pillar of smoke pyramiding into the sky as high as six or more miles as a result of setting off a nuclear blast, who gave that a thought? Now, however, it is seen so often that it is no longer news. This was a development reserved for your day and mine. There is no room for doubt in these important truths. Simultaneously with the outpouring the Spirit comes the signs in heaven and on earth-blood, fire, and smoke. Yet many sit idly by and pay no attention to the importance of our day.

Our day leads to the next great event described in Joel 2:31, "The sun shall be turned into darkness, and the moon into blood, before the great and the terrible day of the Lord comes."

This day is yet in the future and not to be feared by those who are ready to go up with the Lord at the time of the Rapture. But those who refused to prepare will remember that it was written, when it is fulfilled before their eyes.

We are reminded daily of the last day prophecy showing our position relative to the rapture of the church. Seven hundred and thirteen years before Christ came, these words were recorded in Nahum 2:3, 4: "The shield of his mighty men is made red, the valiant men are in scarlet: the chariots shall be with flaming torches in the day of his preparation, and the fir trees shall be terribly shaken. The chariots shall rage in the streets, they shall jostle one against another in the broad ways: they shall seem like torches, they shall run like the lightnings" (Nahum 2:3, 4).

"And when Ye shall see Jerusalem compassed with armies, then know that the desolation thereof is nigh. For are the days of vengeance, that all things which are written may be fulfilled. And there shall be signs in the sun, and in the moon, and in the stars; and upon the earth distress of nations, with perplexity; the sea and the waves roaring. And then shall they see the Son of man coming in a cloud with power and great glory."

The Lord told us in Luke 21:20, 22, 25, 27: Then we shall remember that it was written of Him. The Lord Jesus in a statement recorded in Matthew 5:17, 18, gave His position relative to the Word of God and its fulfillment. He said, "Think not that I am come to destroy the law, or the prophets: I am not come to destroy, but to fulfill. For verily I say unto you, Till heaven and earth pass, one jot or one title shall in no wise ass from the law, till all be fulfilled." No higher authority can speak that He who gave this proclamation. Let men of any degree make their own evaluation of this spoken Word. Yet the prediction in this Book will be seen before the eyes of men to prove that God's Word is yea and amen.

Let us of these last days be mindful of the fact that we are on the threshold of Christ's appearing. The Apostle Paul has given us a preview of the manner of this event in 1 Thessalonians 4:13-18.

l-r   Floyd Timmerman, G. W. Lane, Jimmy Carter

10

Cost of Compromise

*"Thou hast trodden down all them
that err from thy statutes:
for their deceit is falsehood"*

(Psalm 119:118).

Compromise is said to be the sacrificing of one right, or good in the effort of gaining another, too often ending in the loss of both. Generally a compromise is the result of uncertainty, which is the mother of indecision and confusion. This you might be able to afford in anything else, but you cannot afford it in religion. Whether or not you are right in religion determines whether or not you will be happy in eternity. There is no uncertainty in the fact of heaven and hell, even though attacks have been made on the fact of their existence. There is a heaven and there is a hell. This makes it necessary that we know what is right and do nothing but right.

To show willingness to compromise with the principles outlined in the Scripture is only to show that we are in doubt about the authenticity of the Scripture and eternal future. That religion has been dependent upon compromising people for its promotion in the world is a sad fact. There has developed a tendency to treat God's Word and work as something less than first in importance, and to some it has become little more than man's word to produce a social order. When the weakness of humanity causes compromise within our church's operation, you can expect nothing but a powerless church that cannot produce a determination in its people. Defeat is practically assured in such an attitude.

Not a compromise but a definite decision saved baby Moses in spite of the king's decree. A fearful compromising crowd stood back trembling when David with a definite purpose went into the valley to bring back the head of a roaring giant. There was no compromise in Elijah's attitude when he met the challenge of 450 prophets of Baal. It was his definite decision that enabled him to pray down the fire from heaven with sixty-three words. His lack of compromise enabled him to see the sacrifice consumed and every drop of the twelve barrels of water licked up by his answered prayer. It was his uncompromising stand that let him see the subdued look on the face of his challengers while he stood by the altar of a burnt offering and dry trenches.

While everyone was bowing to the graven image at the sound of the music, it took a backbone like a sawlog for the three Hebrew boys to stand straight. But they had it. Consider these men for a moment. Their temptation did not start the moment the music sounded. Their captors had been working on them for a time. But the treatment did not penetrate as they hoped. They, along with Daniel, were men of strong character and not soon shaken. Their description is found in Daniel 1:4, "Children in whom was no blemish, but well favored, and skillful in all wisdom, and cunning in knowledge, and understanding science, and such as had ability in them to stand in the king's palace, and whom they might teach the learning and the tongue of the Chaldeans."

Contrary to the thinking of many people who have the opinion that rigid religion and intelligence do not go together, these men were at the top in both. They were enrolled in school for three years to study the language, and then they were to serve in the palace of the king. They gave Daniel and the three Hebrew boys different names, names of flattery in accordance to their desire for them. They changed Daniel, whose name meant "God's Judge," to Belteshazzar, which means, "favored by Bel, or Baal." Hannaniah, which means, "Whom God graciously gave," was changed to Shadrack, which means "royal, or great scribe." Mishael that means, "Who is what God is, was changed to Meshack, that meant "guest of a king." Azariah meant, "Whom Jehovah aids"; they changed this to "Abednego," which meant "servant or worshiper of Nebo." This will give you an idea of the brainwashing these men went through, but they were not the compromising type. They had the opportunity of fairing sumptuously on the king's rations, but they refused to deviate from their own standard and asked for pulse and water. They did not let their surroundings affect them to the point of yielding against their rule of living. Sure, they were captives but all cautious. If they had started compromising from the start by giving in to flattery or food, they would have been well on their way to bowing to the image with the masses.

Since they had not, they were in good condition to stand to their convictions. Yes, they went through the fire for their stand; but they would not burn for the king. Men with such character will not bow down whether you brag on them, browbeat them, or attempt to burn them. I submit to you that it takes this kind to keep old-time religion alive even in our time.

John the Baptist was a good example of what it takes to bring people to the proper attitude of acceptance of Jesus. He minced no words, nor did he put on an act of diplomacy to gain followers. There was no compromise even hinted in his presentation. He actually told some halfhearted applicants to leave and return only when they could prove their sincerity, but it seems that he had no lack of people to baptize. He was in no way a product of their school of thought. He dressed differently, ate differently, and was in every sense of the word unlike them. But his message was full strength and proved to be the message of the hour. He preached about the Lord until he saw Jesus amid standing the multitudes. They were there because the cities and villages were emptied out as they came to stand on the banks of Jordan to hear this unpolished man preach an uncompromising gospel. He went so far as to call some of the bystanders a generation of vipers and asked them "who hath warned you to flee the wrath to come." We would hardly expect to hear that kind of expression today unless one is willing to lose some of his congregation. Then John was the only preacher who preached Christ. Now you are able to hear whatever suits you, whether right or wrong. There is always someone who will compromise with you because we are living in a day of religious carelessness.

A clear picture of the difference between compromise and conviction is seen in the Apostle Peter. It was the compromise he made with the scoffers at the judgment hall that caused Jesus to turn toward him with a look of sympathy, and the same sent Peter out with bitter tears streaming down his face. This act of weakness caused him such remorse that he refused to die with his head up. They crucified him with his head down. It was a converted Simon Peter that preached with great power and determination on the Day of Pentecost that resulted in the salvation of thousands that day. It was the same strong stand that gave him the anointing that blessed the multitudes thereafter. His shadow passed over sick and afflicted, and they were made well. I would rather live powerfully for a short time than to spend a long lifetime as a spineless weakling as he appeared before his anointing.

One of the things to appreciate about the Apostle Paul is that he had retained his integrity from the beginning. When he was brought before magistrates, judges, governors, kings or religionists, he always had the answer because he had no thought of compromise. No one had a harder time of persecution than he, but his firm stand brought the reward of power in his life. The beatings, stonings, imprisonment or impending death did not deter him from his purpose to preach the gospel. When he heard them grinding the chop block to cut off his head, he wrote these great words, "The time of my departure is at hand. I have fought a good fight, I have finished my course, I have kept the faith: Henceforth there is laid up for me a crown of righteousness" (2 Timothy 4:7, 8). Why should not such a man stand out as the chief promoter for the cause of Christ? He would just as soon die for Christ as live for Him.

Many men and movements have since had the opportunities to compromise the truth, but enough have refused to let the world know the truth of the gospel. Those men whose preaching has meant the most in these days are those whose messages have rung out with pungent, penetrating declaration of the truth of the Pentecostal experience with not a hint of compromise. They have held to their strong conviction, which helped them to stem the tide of public sentiment. Now millions are standing as a monument to their faith and firm decision.

When the little city of Ai defeated the army of Israel, it was a great surprise to Joshua and the leaders. They were so sure of victory that they did not even send the entire army against them. But great was the upset. This defeat threw Joshua and the leaders on their faces in humiliation and despair. If they could not put Ai down, they would surely be without any future success. God told Joshua to get up off his face and investigate the trouble. When the truth was known, it revealed that Chan had disregarded God's commandment to leave all accursed things in Jericho when it fell. He did not go for many things, but he wanted just a small Babylonian garment, some gold and silver. That, he thought, would be a small thing too insignificant to think about; but God would not overlook it. Defeat at Ai meant that many were slain in battle, and the confidence of God's people was greatly damaged. Great was the cost of this compromise.

Achan and all his family were stoned and all his possessions destroyed. Could anyone think the compromise was worth it? A similar incident was seen in King Saul when he was in battle with the Amalekites. God told him to leave everything to be completely destroyed, but Saul thought that he had a better idea. He saw some things that appeared beautiful-some fat cattle and sheep; and as a matter of pride, he brought along the defeated king to feed his personal ego. When he met the Lord's man Samuel, he acted in his usual pious way and testified to his obedience; but he did not fool anyone but himself. Samuel saw all the way through his hypocrisy. The cattle and sheep did not know to keep still, so they testified against him.

At a later date a battle was raging, and Saul was in the heat of the fight. Seeing that death was sure, he fell on his own sword; but he did not complete the job. Along came one of the Amalekites that he had brought along that should have died at the time of the invasion. Saul asked him who was. "I am an Amalekite," was the reply. Saul requested him to kill him. In words of the Amalekite, this was Saul's finish. I stood upon him, and slew him, because was sure that he could not live after that he was fallen: and I took the crown that was upon his head." Think of the shame of this man who stood head and shoulders above all men of the kingdom, now with an enemy standing on him lifting his crown from his head - crowned by God and uncrowned by an Amalekite that he should have destroyed. What a true picture of the cost of compromise!
It will be your story also if you do not rid yourself of your willingness to disobey God as a   compromise in pursuit of your own selfishness.

One of the most tragic stories in the Scripture is that of the mighty and powerful man named Samson. He, of necessity, slew thousands of his enemies single-handed. When it looked as if he were cornered, he carried off the gates of the city. This source of power and strength was in the vow he had made as a Nazarite. His strength depended on the long locks of his hair. He began to court a friend of his Philistine enemies. She was not working for Samson's interest, but he was blinded by his infatuation. She was after his power so that he could be defeated. Step by step he kept coming closer to revealing his secret of power. Even with full knowledge of her attempts to bind him in the presence of his enemies, he continued to give opportunities for complete destruction. Finally he let down all bars and told her that if she cut off the locks of his hair, he would be as any other man. He dropped off to sleep and was shorn of his source of strength. He shook himself only to find himself powerless. His eyes were punched out, and he had to grind at the mill. Finally his hair grew, and he asked God for one last surge of power. A boy led him to a pillar in the palace. As everyone reveled, he slew more with one pull than in his entire life. No one could think his compromise was worth the cost.

I beg you, Christian, for the sake of souls who can be won only through the power of the gospel, to hold fast to the old-fashioned way without trying to give religion a new look. Remember that it is the way of the cross that leads home, and the Word will light the way to Calvary.

GENERAL OFFICES
MEMORANDUM

To: _____ From: _____

Subject: _____ Date: June 1964

Great God and Father of all, the head of man. There is a great need in this land for divine guidance. Our homelife is far from what it should be. The moral standards have been broken down and it look as though, by the day, we can see conditions becoming more dreadful. You are the only one powerful enough to bolster our national homelife. It will take a work of grace. Many have written to us asking prayer for homes just about to be broken, and we do pray for them now. Lay your loving hand upon those homes that are in danger now and impart love strong enough to sustain. When homes are torn asunder hearts are broken and families are scattered and the devil has a stronger chance to wreck every life. Please hear us today and grant our petition in Christ name

Handwritten prayer for radio broadcast

11

Lift of Life

"He raiseth up the poor out of the dust, and lifteth the needy out of the dunghill; that he may set him with princes, even with the princes of his people."

-Psalm 113:7, 8

A cry comes from fallen humanity sunken deep in despondency and despair inquiring, "How can I find a way out of my troubles and make life worth living?" To this question many answers are given and as many have failed; so humanity goes on needing a lift. Some have sought to be helped by a change of environment, others through education and cultural attainments, while there are those who, by fighting their way through life, seek to find a degree of satisfaction, and a much-attempted method is that of revelry and excitement of night life in an endeavor to throw off the disappointments and despondency of their fallen state. A quick glance across our own nation will show us to what extend these efforts have been successful.

Come with me into New York, the nation's largest city, which seems to be a melting pot of people from every nation. These people have come into this land of opportunity in search of a new life away from bondage, poverty and fear. They hoped to be lifted from their low plane of living.

One does not have to be a close observer to see that there is much disappointment to some as they fail in their pursuit. The look on the face of the man who pushes the two-wheeled cart gathering papers and junk of all descriptions in an effort to seek out a bare living shows that life is not very pleasant, and true happiness is far from being realized. Visit the slum section of this or any other city where you can watch the small boys and girls as they play in the streets with others who have had no better opportunity than they had; then go with them as they return to their homes where unchurched parents provide an atmosphere of loose living which tends to add much to their sure disappointment in the future lives of their offspring. This doesn't provide a lift.

Let us travel into the nation's capitol, Washington, D.C., into which city we send our most distinguished citizens from every state in the Union. They, in turn, surround themselves with the most qualified workers available from an educational and cultural standpoint. Likewise, the nations of the world send their most polished diplomats to represent them. This makes Washington a great city of learning and dignity. If these attributes could cure the aching heart and soothe the troubled mind, this city would be a heaven on earth, but even in this atmosphere of high-class living there is anxiety, fear and discontentment, which leads some to take their own lives as they come face to face with the problems of life.

Go from here to Lake Success, New York, where the representatives of the United Nations exercise their intellectual skill in the effort to lift the world into a realm of peace. But even among these master minds of the world we hear of those who, when faced with realities of life, give up in despair and leap from skyscrapers or destroy themselves in some other way. By this we readily conclude that education or cultural attainment does not give the needed lift.

Take a look into another of our largest cities. This one seems to be noted for its connection with many vices. Here we find the huddling of hoodlums, who could be from any section of any city, or from any walk of life.

These people are known as the underworld, or gangsters. They are in hiding from their past lives. They feel they are being sought or followed and that their past is about to overtake them. Disappointments in life have driven them to hate the world as they look upon it from a warped point of view. They know they can go no lower, and they see no way to rise higher, so in their desperation they charge the world with a living for themselves and hope to get it by any possible means. For this reason, the nation stands in fear of them. The individual history of these people would be very interesting if we had the opportunity to know it. Among these people you would find some bankers, lawyers, doctors, politicians, merchants, and men and women from every walk of life.

Theirs is the idea to put up a fight with life in order to get what they desire or to even a score in order to satisfy a despondent feeling; but when their past overtakes them and they put up their last fight usually there is a volley of bullets and shedding of blood and a man is left lying on the street to prove to all that fighting life does not bring about the desired lift.

As a last visit let us go to Hollywood, the film capitol of the world. Here you will find the most glamorous, the most talented, and the best trained people of the world whose personal attributes provide for them the most luxurious living one could desire having everything money can buy. This being true many have sought a career in movies and on stage, hoping that when they have reached their goal and their ambition is realized the bright lights, the gaiety of night life, the admiration of viewers, and plenty of money to provide a high-class living that life would hold no problems for them and they would never have a care. Yet the discontentment, the heartbreaks and personal failures among these people would not be a recommendation for theirs as a life that would give the needed lift.

Disappointments and restlessness, as stated before, have driven men of every walk of life to seek relief, and comfort by drowning their true feelings in excessive drink, or to seek an artificial feeling of greatness by the use of dope. Thus a great percentage of the world's population, from the banker to the garbage collector, has been given to this practice which has degraded and reduced men to instability of character and complete uselessness. It is not unusual to see men of high standing in former days whose lives have been ruined by reckless living in search of happiness or excitement.

A picture of the foregoing is very plainly shown in the Scripture in the life of a young man for whom life seemed to hold everything, but as he sat in the calm security of his father's home his ambition ran wild; his thoughts were of the gaiety of night life in the city, prosperity, a big name, excitement and fun of the life of revelry. He requested his father to make a settlement with him and let him go into the world for himself. This request being granted, he went in pursuit of this new and different life; spending his fortune, making and losing friends, living a life of dissipation in night spots, amusement halls, and drunkenness, no doubt thinking, "This is the life," until finally "he had spent all." He had nothing left including the friends he had gained. All had vanished. Nothing remained but the cold hard fact that he had come to the end of his exciting life, and a question was forcing itself upon him, "What now?"

With the young man, known as "the prodigal son," went all the above disappointed people to the "far country," and they were next seen at the swine pen feeding the swine, in the land of despondency. All who land there live in a stupor of despair.

No doubt the first few days after his arrival at the swine pen the memories of the recent exciting days afforded some pleasant thought, but the days passed on and on until these faded away and present realities made life hard. We can imagine him as looking neat and well kept upon his arrival, but now long hair, unshaven, worn-out clothes, sandals torn to shreds, a completely changed man- a man without money, without love, without excitement, without social standing, without character. "He had spent all."

I am glad the account of this young man's life doesn't end on such a sad note. There is a thrill that goes through our hearts as we watch him, and one day we hear him ask a question of himself: "How many hired servants of my father's have bread enough and to spare, and I perish with hunger?" And with a determination he exclaims, "'I will arise and go to my father, and say unto him, I have sinned against heaven and before thee,' and I will ask for the privilege to stay at home, even as a servant."

In the story of his penitent young man we can see him stand upon his feet, dust his unkempt clothes, run his hand through his uncombed hair and stroke his unshaven face. A gleam in his eye tells that he remembers from whence he came, and picking up the few remaining rags he has, he bids farewell to the land of despondency and we watch as he walks out of sight, headed for home.

Now we stand at the front of a well arranged home and see an old father as he anxiously watches the road. He appears to be hoping for someone's arrival. A traveler comes into view, walking with tired but determined gait. The old father catches a glimpse and looks in the direction of the traveler as one who watches with hope for someone. He looks long – he leans forward – and now he is going with speed toward the traveler.

It's the "prodigal son" on the home stretch. Now they meet and embrace. The son is welcomed. The servants are called; new clothes are provided; a feast is prepared; a dance is arranged; a festive occasion is on because of a glorious comeback made by a wayward son.

Jesus, on one occasion, entered Samaria and visited Jacob's well in the hope of refreshing himself after a long journey. He saw a woman of that city as she approached the well carrying a water pot, which task had been hers all of her lifetime.

A study of her past revealed that she was a woman of many disappointments. She had had five husbands and her present companion was not one of the five. In the eyes of anyone she would be a very undesirable character. Possibly she was aware that she was considered as such. When Jesus spoke to her, she could hardly understand why He would break the tradition of standing aloof. She said, "How is it that thou, being a Jew, asketh drink of me which am a woman of Samaria, for the Jews have no dealings with the Samaritans?" Jesus answered and said, "If thou knewest the gift of God, and who it is that saith to thee, Give me to drink; thou wouldest have asked of him, and he would have given thee living water."

This woman, accustomed to drawing water from the well, could not comprehend His message of living water. She said, "Sir, you have nothing to draw with, and the well is deep: from whence then hast thou that living water? Art thou greater than our father Jacob, which gave us this well, and drank thereof himself, and his children, and his cattle?"

The answer Jesus gave this disappointed, disillusioned woman should give hope to every man or woman whose life has been filled with a thirst for the beggarly things of the world, which has no satisfaction to offer; the man who is driven by inner cravings to drink and do drugs, who hates himself after every fling and foolishness which threw him into the gutter to be looked upon with scorn by those who passed him by, but who "thirsts again," and over and over is conquered and thrown by raving desires, Jesus said, "Whosoever drinketh of the water that I shall give him shall never thirst."

The Samaritan woman, no doubt, took a quick glimpse back through her life at the struggles and defeat she has suffered through her inner cravings and desires which had led her into many disappointments but now hope springs up within her soul.

One drink of this living water will cleanse and deliver me and satisfy me. She says, "Sir, give me this water." Immediately she dropped her water pot as she realized the springing up of living water, refreshing, thrilling and satisfying. She took the promised well and went to town telling all the people she met and all who up to this time find themselves in her former condition, "Come, see a man who told me all."

We are told of another man in the Scripture to whom life had passed by, through no fault of his own, except that he was unable to carry himself. He lacked strength to travel so he was placed by others by the side of the path where he was able to see the people pass by, and where he could beg a scant living for himself by extending his tin cup. This he had done throughout his life.

He was sitting at the gate of the Temple called "Beautiful" but possibly had never passed through to the house of worship. It is likely that he had never asked anyone to carry him through to see the beauties and splendor of God's house; so his thoughts and imagination and ambitions were no higher than his living – a wayside existence.

Everyone knows someone whose life is very uneventful. He doesn't accumulate friends; he doesn't have money; he doesn't own property; he doesn't seem to be anxious to improve his standing, or to make a success of anything. He doesn't seem to care for the excitement of crowded night clubs; he doesn't get farther than the corner saloon; he doesn't give a thought of going to church or seeing that his children go to Sunday School; as a matter of fact, he doesn't know what it is to really live. His is a wayside existence.

Peter and John had started to the Temple at the hour of prayer and had gotten as far as "the gate called Beautiful," where sat the man by the side of the road. He, with an anxious eye looked at them and extended his cup, as usual, as if to say, "A small coin, nothing large. I don't expect much. Mine is a tin-cup existence."

"And Peter, fastening his eyes upon him with John, said, Look on us." Look on us; we were at one time seaside dwellers. Look on us; we haven't always traveled among men. Look on us; we know what it is to be disappointed. Look on us; we have fished nights at a time and caught nothing. Look on us; we were lonely, but Jesus came our way. Look on us; our lives are filled with excitement and great joy.

He gave heed unto them, expecting to receive something, and he was not going to be disappointed, even thought he was talking to a man who said, "Silver and gold have I none." This same man was able to say, "'But such as I have, give I thee,' I have an acquaintance with Jesus, and you are going to benefit by it. I have an anointing by the Holy Ghost, and you are going to feel it. I have a desire to give you a lift, and you are going to get it."

He took him by the hand and lifted him up, and immediately his feet and ankle bones received strength. The man leaped up, stood, and walked, and entered with them into the Temple walking and leaping and praising God. No doubt this man said, "No more sitting by the side of the road, no more reaching my tin cup to those who pass on by, because I have received the lift of life.

The needed lift for fallen humanity does not come through a change of environment, educational or cultural attainment, giving ourselves to revelry, or lighthearted living, but it is found in our contract with the Lord Jesus Christ.

> *"This poor man cried, and the Lord heard him,*
> *and saved him out of all his troubles."*
> *-Psalm 34:6*

"Voice of Calvary" radio broadcast
12th & Elm, Cincinnati, OH

12

This Waiting World

"And they asked him, saying, Master, but when shall these things be?"

Luke 21: 7.

The world has had waiting periods throughout all its known history. There was the time when God had judged the people and declared there would be a flood to destroy everything on the face of the earth. The people were warned, but they did not believe. Nevertheless, it was a fact and Noah's being the only one who believed did not excuse the rest or exempt them from their destruction. They were all swept away. When God makes up a schedule and makes the proclamation to the world, it happens just as He says, and it does not miss the schedule whether it is a thousand years, a day, or a split second.

Ever since God had made it known that He would send a Deliverer to redeem the world from sin, the world had waited. They expected to hear of Him at any time. They waited. Every outstanding baby was looked upon with hope and anticipation. Maybe he would be the Messiah. When a prophet would show exceptional ability the world watched Him. I imagine when Elijah prayed and obtained dust, rain, and fire, the people expected to hear that he was their deliverer. They longed for deliverance from their bondage of sin, and were weary in waiting.

When John the Baptist began to preach, "The Kingdom of heaven is at hand," that sounded like the message for which they had been waiting. When he called upon them to repent, they knew he was preparing them for the great event. He from else looked and acted so different everyone they were sure he was the man. When they inquired of him, he answered, "I am not the Christ; I am the voice of one crying in the wilderness, Make straight the way of the Lord, as said the prophet Esaias." Thrills went through their hearts as he continued, "I baptize with water: but there standees one among you, whom ye know not: he it is, who coming after me is preferred before me, whose shoe's latchet I am not worthy to unloose" (John 1:20, 23, 26, 27).

Then came the moment for which they had waited. John cried out, "Behold the Lamb of God which teeth away the sin of the world." A silence fell upon the crowd as all anxiously awaited the presentation of their Lord. Jesus broke the silence by starting for the water and announcing that He desired baptism. John consented reluctantly because of his feeling of unworthiness.

When the baptism was finished and Jesus came straightway up out of the water, the waiting multitudes had reason to rejoice as God the Father spoke and said, "This is my beloved Son, in whom I am well pleased." At that moment the Holy Ghost descended upon Him in the form of a dove. There, before their very eyes, was the inaugural ceremony of the Lord Jesus Christ with heaven and earth both in participation. This was worth all the worlds waiting. No one else has ever had such acclaim. Coronations and inaugurations are attended and honored by royalty and diplomats from neighboring nations, but never has God made another introduction and presentation.

This was not an inauguration of an earthly king, but of a Missionary from another world. "He came not to be ministered unto, but to minister," reconciling to the world to God His Father, and to proclaim the gospel story of good news to the world. The people were hoping for a king, and Christ's presentation was not acceptable to them. They crucified Him out of an unwillingness to accept a Saviour. When they put Him in the tomb the world thought they were through with Him, but they were not. They were just waiting again. They did not know it, but He was to be seen again walking the streets of the city. The world was waiting for Him with or without its consent.

He was in their midst a resurrected Christ, not a Christ with spittle on His face or a reed in His hand; not standing quietly as a lamb, or in physical weakness, trembling. That was all on the other side of the grave through which He had passed. He had gone through and whipped out all the human affliction it could impose upon Him, and now stood as one impossible to touch with human or devilish conspiracy. He had successfully put down all the work of their hands and was walking among them to prove it. He gave the world a picture in miniature of a future event by bringing with Him from the dead, some of their old acquaintances. For forty days He walked with His disciples and gave them finishing touches of His doctrine, and tasks to be carried out by the church after His ascension.

The time came for His return to the Father in heaven, and He led His followers as far as Bethany. Before their eyes He ascended higher and higher until a cloud received Him out of their sight. They stood gazing toward the heavens hoping to get another glimpse of Him and expecting Him to return immediately. When they heard of this, the enemies of Christ again hoped that they would have no word from Him and that they could get back to a normal operation. What they did not know was that Jesus said, "I to go prepare a place for you. And if I go. . . I will come again, and receive you unto myself; that where I am, there ye may be also" (John 14:2, 3). Neither did they know that the angel of the Lord appeared to the disciples at Bethany and said to them, "Why stand ye gazing up into heaven? This same Jesus, which is taken up from you into heaven, shall so come in like manner as ye have seen him go into heaven" (Acts 1:11).

This again puts us in a position as a waiting world. It is true that we have been waiting a long time and some are asking the question, "Where is the promise of his coming? Since our fathers fell asleep all things continue as from the beginning." Impatience is in evidence and doubts arise in the minds of some. Materialism has overtaken many, and the fact of His return is fading out of their thinking. This will not stop Him or delay Him. He will return with or without the interest of the world.

Jesus knew this and gave us admonition to help sustain us in the time of waiting. We are told, "Unto them who look for him shall appear the second time without sin unto Salvation." His appearance will be to those who look for Him, but the disappearance of the Church will be known by all. The world will be affected in a most unusual way. Whether we think of this event once a year or never think of it, every man is included in it one way or another, not by his own arrangement but by arrangements made by the Lord. There is no way around it.

While the world waits, many things take place that affect the thinking of the people. Like Jacob who lost sight of Bethel in his memory and became susceptible to many misgivings in his time of trouble, so the minds of men are being preyed upon today because of their dim view of Christ's return. Christ knew this would happen and gave instruction to help us guard against the wiles of the devil and false teachers. He tells us not to be deceived by those who would come in His name saying they are Christ. When this happens, Jesus declares, the time is near.

Deceit is one of the most effective tools the devil could possibly use on man. It makes wrong appear right, and in the person's own thinking he is right. This is the reason men will fight and die for such erroneous teaching as communism and other false dogmas. The most radical fight is usually put on by those who are deceived. The sad result of this will be those who are led astray through their efforts and will know the truth too late.

During this time of waiting there will be wars and commotions. The Lord said, "Be not terrified." The thoughts uppermost in the minds of our national leaders are of war and world distress. Preparedness for the defense of our country and those allied with us is the central theme of conferences by those responsible. These facts have sent men into suicide as a means of escape. They see no way out, and there is a small chance unless we depend upon God. For the Christian, however, there is no need to be terrified. It is true that death might come, but that would mean an opportunity to see Jesus.

The Lord has a certain schedule for the world, however, which would make it totally impossible for the whole earth to be devastated at this time. Though we wait, we can wait with an inward peace that cannot be disturbed by the world's commotions. The Lord is our refuge and He said, "The end is not by and by" (Luke 21:9). There is plenty of reason naturally, for men to be terrified as the war clouds gather, if he has no hope of escape through Christ. The Lord admonished us in Luke 21:14, "Settle it therefore in your hearts, not to meditate before what ye shall answer," when we are brought before those who are against us as we wait. He had promised to give the answer to the questions and bring the adversaries to naught. "Be not anxious" is His suggestion. Let our case rest in His hands; we cannot solve our problems without Him anyway.

While we wait we must watch our affections and as Christ warned in Luke 21:34, "take heed to yourselves, lest at any time your hearts be overcharged with surfeiting, and drunkenness, and cares of this life, and so that day come upon you unawares." To become careless and too concerned with our natural living and forget God is the real danger which confronts us today - getting too busy to acknowledge God, too busy to worship the Lord; letting the cares of life crowd the church out of our thinking.

"Watch . . . and pray always, that ye may be accounted worthy to escape all these things that shall come to pass, and to stand before the Son of man (Luke 21:36). Herein is stated the solution to the Christian's problem. Watch for the means of escape, which is the coming of the Lord. This is the next event for which the world awaits – when "the Lord himself shall descend from heaven with a shout, with the voice of the archangel, and with the trump of God: and the dead in Christ shall rise first: then we which are alive and remain shall be caught up together with them in the clouds, to meet the Lord in the air: and so shall we ever be with the Lord. Wherefore comfort one another with these words" (1 Thessalonians 4:16-18).

The joy of this waiting is in the fact that we do not know when it will occur. It could be in the next moment or it could be a few years. The suffering child of God rests in the hope that his suffering could be cut short in a moment's time, and at the most it cannot be long. The mileposts of prophecy have all been passed. The known signs we are to expect have all been seen.

To watch for Christ's coming is like waiting at the station for a train at train time. You have the feeling that now is the time. Every new day gives us the feeling that this may be the day.

We live in a state of expectancy. Such a life is a comfort and a thrill. I am reminded of Job, the man in the Scripture who was greatly afflicted, a man who had great faith in the Lord as his Deliverer. As he sat on the heap of ashes scratching himself with the potsherd, he cried out to God, "All the days of my appointed time will I wait, till my change comes. Thou shalt call and I will answer." What a hope belongs to the Christian as we wait for the promised return of our Lord!

The following was composed by Barton Green at his grandfather's desk the day after G. W. Lane's passing, and was revised for Lane's 2004 Induction into the "Hall of Prophets."

"Just came by to tell ya,"
that's how he always began.
Then he'd rub his legs and shake his fist
and tell of God's redemption plan.

His words were always simple
and painted pictures that seemed so real.
You could reach out with that widowed woman,
and the Master's garment you could feel.

Children would smile and take notice
of Mr. Noah and his Ark,
and the old would be inspired when
he'd tell of Job's second start.

When it came time to sing,
he could be heard above the rest,
and though he thought others were better,
"The Bishop" was the best.

He never spoke ill of others,
and when wronged he always forgave.
He cared nothing for competition,
only that lives were saved.

Though he was a son, a brother, a husband,
and father to a special few,
He became a part of every family he ministered to.

But to me, he was simply "Papaw,"
my Grampa, my friend.
And I can find no better role model
if I searched to time's end.

For a generation his frame has laid under earthly sod.
But though the skin worms have devoured his body,
Yet... he is remembered
Yet... he is loved still

And his words will... live... on.

In G. W.'s last book, he projected *Lord Strike My Strings* as the title of his next book to be offered in the building of Lane's Library. Global will honor this effort and produce a book which will consist of radio and TV sermons. The subjects included will be in keeping with the central theme "Living a harmonious life based on the Word of God."

<u>www.gea-books.com</u>

www.ingramcontent.com/pod-product-compliance
Lightning Source LLC
Chambersburg PA
CBHW030141170426
43199CB00008B/161